SEC Football

SEC Football

How a Regional League Became a National Obsession

Colby Newton

ROWMAN & LITTLEFIELD
Lanham • Boulder • New York • London

Published by Rowman & Littlefield
An imprint of The Rowman & Littlefield Publishing Group, Inc.
4501 Forbes Boulevard, Suite 200, Lanham, Maryland 20706
www.rowman.com

86-90 Paul Street, London EC2A 4NE, United Kingdom

British Library Cataloguing in Publication Information Available

Library of Congress Cataloging-in-Publication Data
Names: Newton, Colby, author.
Title: SEC football : how a regional league became a national obsession / Colby Newton.
Other titles: Southeastern Conference football
Description: Lanham, Maryland : Rowman & Littlefield, [2024] | Includes bibliographical
    references. | Summary: "The official slogan for the SEC is "It just means more." And they are
    right. SEC football means more passion, more money, and more titles. This book explores how
    the SEC went from a regional league to a nationwide brand that dominates the college football
    landscape."—Provided by publisher.
Identifiers: LCCN 2023056757 (print) | LCCN 2023056758 (ebook) | ISBN 9781538186947
    (cloth) | ISBN 9781538186954 (epub)
Subjects: LCSH: Southeastern Conference—History. | Football—Southern States—History. |
    Football—Records—Southern States.
Classification: LCC GV958.5.S59 N49 2024 (print) | LCC GV958.5.S59 (ebook) | DDC
    796.330975—dc23/eng/20231227
LC record available at https://lccn.loc.gov/2023056757
LC ebook record available at https://lccn.loc.gov/2023056758

To Amy and my five wonderful children: believe it or not, I love you more than I love SEC football.

To Steve: this book doesn't happen without you. Thank you for everything.

Contents

AUTHOR'S NOTE

The state of Utah in the 1970s and 1980s was a basketball mecca. The local college teams, led by the University of Utah, had a rich history of success on the hardwood. The National Basketball Association (NBA) became a prominent fixture in the community when the Jazz moved from New Orleans to call Salt Lake City home in 1979. The dominant religion in the state, the Church of Jesus Christ of Latter-day Saints, also known as the Mormon Church, built a cultural hall inside most of their churches. The hall was actually a full-court basketball surface, and the church regularly held tournaments for their local communities that members of the congregations took great pride in. This was the culture I was raised in, born in the suburbs of Salt Lake City in December 1976. I grew up loving and playing all sports, including basketball. But my passion, my obsession really, was football, and from as early as I can remember, that passion centered on the Southeastern Conference (SEC).

The first football player I fell in love with was Herschel Walker, the great Heisman-winning running back from Georgia. The notebook from my year in kindergarten, which I still possess, is full of drawings of the Georgia Bulldog "G" logo. Bo Jackson became a larger-than-life figure on my television set as he ran through defenses all over the South on his way to capturing the Heisman.

By the time I reached high school, I followed the SEC closer than any other conference, including the Pac-10, which was the most popular conference on the West Coast. Nearing my sixteenth birthday, I was scheduled for my driving test on the same day as the inaugural SEC Championship Game. It was an event I could not miss! Initially, I pleaded to have my exam rescheduled. With basketball season in full swing in Utah, my explanation about why the SEC was so important received nothing but a puzzled look, and the request was denied. I resolved to record the game on a VHS tape and set out to take my test. As soon as I got into the car, I asked the driving instructor if we could turn the radio on. "You can't have music playing during the test," he said. I explained that I wanted to listen to the SEC title game. Again, a puzzled look, followed by a denial of my request, occurred. After the test (I passed, barely) I rushed home, praying that my recording was intact, and settled in to watch the game that changed college football.

My high school football playing days didn't lead to a scholarship offer from an SEC school, and I hung up my cleats for good. In college, I started a website devoted to covering college football. This was the early days of the internet, and the site provided me with an opportunity to stay close to my love of the sport and the SEC. After predicting (correctly I might add) that the Auburn team of 2003 would perform far beneath their preseason expectations, I had my first experiences directly with the passionate fans of the SEC. When my projections were published, my in-box was instantly filled with colorful remarks letting me know how wrong I was. I loved it!

With the website not paying the bills, I decided it was time to get a real job and began working for a company that was in the bowl game industry. Standing on the sidelines of the 2007 and 2011 Bowl Championship Series (BCS) National Championship games are experiences I will never forget. Watching Louisiana State University (LSU) and Alabama win national titles in person only furthered my passion for the SEC.

For my entire adult life, Saturday afternoons have been built around watching the SEC on CBS. Hearing the iconic theme music to begin the broadcast meant the best part of my week was about to start.

In the summer of 2020, COVID-19 had changed all of our lives and impacted the coming college football season. No one was sure if games would be played. On vacation in Pensacola, Florida, with my family, I noticed an older gentleman at the pool. He was likely in his sixties, wearing a tattered ball cap and a well-worn Alabama Crimson Tide T-shirt. I struck up a conversation, and he told me about his life in the state of

Alabama. As he and I wrapped up our commiseration about the current state of the world, he made a declaration that will stick in my mind forever. In his perfect southern drawl, he said to me, "We have *got* to have football!" As he walked away, I could hear him say it again, this time a bit quieter, to no one in particular. It was almost as if he was sending a prayer up to the heavens. "We've *got* to have football."

To people not only in the South but also across the country, SEC football doesn't just mean more. It means everything.

CHAPTER 1

A Tradition Is Born

THE HEARTBEAT OF COLLEGE FOOTBALL IS IN THE SOUTH. NOWHERE else is the passion and pageantry greater. But the game so many Americans love and so many in the South proclaim as their religion was actually born in the Northeast. In the years immediately following the Civil War, the first schools to field teams were part of the so-called Ivy League. The very first college football game took place in New Jersey in 1869 between Princeton and Rutgers. The first coach to earn national acclaim and who is now recognized as the father of American football, Walter Camp, coached at Yale, located in New Haven, Connecticut.

As the sport increased in popularity in the late 1800s, it also increased in geography as more schools began to field teams. In the early twentieth century, the University of Michigan, coached by Fielding H. Yost, and the University of Chicago, coached by Amos Alonzo Stagg, rose to national prominence. The University of Pittsburgh, led by coach Glenn "Pop" Warner, won 30 consecutive games between 1915 and 1918. A few years later, a little-known Catholic school in northern Indiana took the college football world by storm. Knute Rockne and his Notre Dame Fighting Irish won three national titles in the early 1920s and became known for their barnstorming ways, playing any team, anywhere.

Going as far back as 1869, national championships in college football were handed out by various organizations whose members voted on which team deserved the honor or by a mathematical formula that had been devised. At times, as many as six schools per season lay claim to the national championship, with many of those titles awarded retroactively. From 1869 through the 1924 season, 120 national champions were crowned. Only seven of those titles went to teams in the South: LSU (1908), Auburn (1913), Georgia Tech—notably coached by John Heisman (1916, 1917), Georgia (1920), and Vanderbilt (1921, 1922).

As college football passed its fiftieth anniversary, schools in the South were given little respect when compared to their counterparts in the North and the Midwest. In order for that perception to change, a team would need to emerge not only as a dominant program regionally but also as one that would compete on the national stage.

Enter the University of Alabama.

In 1912, George Hutcheson "Mike" Denny was hired as the new president of the University of Alabama. The school had fewer than 600 students, no paved roads or sidewalks, and only nine major buildings on campus when he began his tenure. By the time he was forced to retire due to poor health in 1936, the university had more than 5,000 students (including more than 1,200 women—up from 55 when he took the helm) and 23 major buildings, many of which still serve as the center of campus to this day.

Paramount to the growth of the school was the priority Denny placed on athletics in general and the football program specifically. Before Denny was named president, Alabama won as many games as they lost. The fortunes began to improve when Denny made the controversial decision to name a former horse racing reporter, Xen Scott, as the head coach in 1919. The team was successful immediately, going 29–9–3 in four seasons under Scott. In 1920, in recognition of the new prosperity on the gridiron, the stadium name was changed from University Field to Denny Field. But it wasn't until Scott retired from his coaching position before the 1923 season that Denny was given the opportunity to lay the foundation for Alabama to become the national power it is today.

As Denny searched for the successor to Xen Scott, he came across Wallace Wade, at the time an assistant at Vanderbilt University and a Tennessee native. In the early 1920s, Vanderbilt had established itself as the premier program in the South under head coach Dan McGugin. The Commodores posted undefeated records in 1921 and 1922 and retroactively claimed shares of national championships both seasons. In 1923, they won the Southern Conference title with an overall record of 5–2–1 and ended the season by hosting a game for charity with northern power Princeton.

With the success that Vanderbilt was experiencing, Alabama wasn't the only school looking to hire Wade, who had become a hot prospect to take over his own program as head coach. Conference rival Kentucky was also aiming to hire the Vanderbilt assistant and name him their head coach. Wade was invited to travel to Kentucky before Alabama could get to him, and he met with the search committee in Lexington. After speaking with members of the university administration, he was asked to wait nearby for a decision to be made regarding a job offer. But the committee deliberated for nearly three hours, and the mercurial Wade became furious at the indecisiveness with which he had been met. He charged back into the room and declared to all parties involved that he not only was going to take the job at Alabama but also would never lose a game to Kentucky as long as he was running a program.[1]

Wallace Wade ended up being a head coach in college football for 24 years. His teams played Kentucky 11 times. They didn't lose once.

Beginning his tenure in 1923, Wade had an instant and profound impact on Alabama football. As a former star player at Brown University, he participated in the Rose Bowl in 1917 and learned early on what it took to compete at the college level. He won a conference title in his second season in Tuscaloosa and by his third season had built a legitimate powerhouse. Playing a nine-game schedule in the 1925 campaign, Alabama dispatched every one of their opponents with overwhelming superiority. Not only did the Crimson Tide go unbeaten, but they also gave up only one touchdown all year and in the process claimed another Southern Conference championship, giving them back-to-back titles. But in a surprising development, their year was about to go from remarkable to unprecedented, as it did not end with the final regular season game.

The Tournament of Roses hosted their first football game in 1902, but the result was a blowout, with Michigan beating Stanford so badly that Stanford quit the game in the third quarter. For the next 14 years, the Tournament of Roses decided to host other contests to entertain the spectators, including chariot and ostrich races. Football returned to the event for good in 1916, and within the next few years, the Rose Bowl game caught the attention of the sports world. The Rose Bowl stadium was completed in time to host the game on January 1, 1923, and it was the only bowl game in the country at the time.

By 1925, some of the more prominent schools in the eastern United States began feeling pressure from the American Association of University Professors that academics were taking a back seat to athletics. As the Tournament of Roses committee looked for a worthy opponent for the University of Washington for the game on January 1, 1926, they were having trouble securing a team. Colgate, Dartmouth, and Yale all turned down invitations. Officials reluctantly turned to Alabama, handing the university the very first bowl bid for a southern team.

With a travel itinerary of five days on a train to get to Pasadena, including a stop at the Grand Canyon, and little respect nationally for southern football, Alabama wasn't given much of a chance in their first Rose Bowl. Falling behind, 12–0, in the first half didn't change that perception. Wade stormed into the locker room at halftime and shouted, "They told me boys from the South would fight" and marched back out.[2]

Inspired by their coach and led by halfback Johnny Mack Brown and quarterback Pooley Hubert, Alabama refused to give up, eventually clawing their way to an improbable 20–19 victory. Football in the South had been changed forever, and the jubilation was felt all over the region. On the train ride back to Tuscaloosa, as the team rode through town after town, brass bands hailed the heroes. As the train pulled into the station for a stop in New Orleans, nearly 1,000 Tulane students surrounded the tracks to serenade the victors.[3]

Southern historian Wayne Flint commented, "If Alabama had lost badly in 1926 by 40 points or more would football then have become the sort of important defining experience that it became over the next five decades? My answer is no. It would not have. Because the south would have just been proved yet again to be inferior in some other dimension in life."[4]

"You can look at the 1926 Rose Bowl as the most significant event in Southern football history," said Andrew Doyle, a history professor at

Winthrop University who has written about the sport. "What had come before was almost like a buildup, a preparation for this grand coming out party. And it was a sublime tonic for Southerners who were buffeted by a legacy of defeat, military defeat, a legacy of poverty, and a legacy of isolation from the American political and cultural mainstream."[5]

Alabama was named the national champions in 1925 and followed that magical campaign with another unbeaten season and a trip to the Rose Bowl in 1927. They tied powerful Stanford, 7–7, in the game but did enough to be named the national champions again. Just four years after arriving as the head coach, Wallace Wade won consecutive national titles. It would be the first of four times Alabama would accomplish the feat.

Back-to-back titles would be difficult to live up to, and the next three seasons did not meet the suddenly high standards that had been set in Tuscaloosa. The Tide lost at least three games each year. Wade felt undervalued and disrespected and announced prior to the 1930 season that he would be leaving for Duke University. With suddenly lofty expectations now in place, Wade found himself in a circumstance that presaged what many future Alabama head coaches would face. Wade agreed to stay on for one final season and promptly led Alabama to another unbeaten record and a national title.

In 1980, the University of Alabama brought many of the players and coaches from the 1930 team back to campus to honor their accomplishments. When 88-year-old Wallace Wade was introduced to the current Tide players, the Alabama head coach at the time said, "Men, I'd like you to meet Coach Wallace Wade, the man who is most responsible for the University of Alabama football tradition. In many ways he is the reason I'm here and the reason you're here."[6]

* * *

The Alabama teams of the late 1920s laid the foundation for college football in the South to flourish. In 1931, another southern school made the trip to Pasadena to compete in the Rose Bowl, when Tulane faced the University of Southern California (USC). With the notoriety of multiple appearances in the biggest game in college football, the sport became more popular in southern communities. And with that, it also became more important to the universities that sponsored football.

The Southern Conference was formed in 1921 with 14 institutions but quickly grew to 23 schools in 11 different states by the end of the 1920s. Disagreements had begun to creep in among members of the group, including a ban on games played on the first Saturday after Thanksgiving (the rule was suspended). Filming games for scouting purposes was not allowed. Radio broadcasts were outlawed in 1931 in the hopes of boosting attendance at games. With the conference covering such a wide range of geography, travel costs became a hindrance to many athletic departments.

On December 9, 1932, with the country mired in the great depression, member schools of the Southern Conference held their annual meeting at the Andrew Johnson Hotel in Knoxville, Tennessee. In the afternoon session, Dr. S. V. Sanford, president of the University of Georgia, served notice to the Southern Conference that the 13 programs west and south of the Appalachian Mountains would be breaking away and creating a new conference. A vote was taken to see if a committee needed to be formed, and by a 17–6 margin, the resolution passed to deliberate on the notice. With little in the way to preclude the fracture from taking place, the meeting adjourned with the decision to split up the conference.

President John J. Tigert of the University of Florida released a statement shortly after and said, in part, "Since in our judgment the time has arrived for a more compact organization for the administration of athletics, it seems wise for a division of the Southern Conference to be made solely on geographical lines. The thirteen institutions in the states of Alabama, Florida, Georgia, Kentucky, Louisiana, Mississippi, and Tennessee hereby tender their resignations as members of the Southern Conference and organize themselves in the Southeastern Conference. . . . The real reason for this organization is a desire to form a conference of institutions in the same geographical territory."[7]

The newly formed conference members included Alabama, Auburn, Florida, Georgia, Georgia Tech, Kentucky, LSU, Ole Miss, Mississippi State, Sewanee, Tennessee, Tulane, and Vanderbilt.

With rivalries broken and longtime relationships severed, the *Knox-ville Journal* lamented the new conference. "The ten remaining members of the Southern Conference—those fine institutions that have always formed the northern group will no longer be forced to contend with a web of politics. The 'politicians' if you will pardon me saying so, are now where they belong—in ONE group."[8]

The SEC was born.

Frank McVey, president of the University of Kentucky, was elected the first president of the SEC. Athletics were immediately placed at the forefront of each member institution. The bylaws for the new conference read, in part, "The Southeastern Conference is organized to form a group of institutions with similar education ideals . . . and increase their ability to render the services for which they were founded, by making athletics part of the education plan." Unlike previous arrangements, the SEC quickly established each school president as the primary representative to the conference.[9]

College athletics in the early twentieth century was filled with plenty of colorful characters but with very little regulation. Athletic scholarships did not exist. When it came to recruiting and compensating players, it was all done under the table so as to not tarnish the amateur athlete.

"The Big Ten and West Coast schools weren't giving outright scholarships, but they were giving jobs sweeping the snow off the front walkway of the Coliseum in Los Angeles, where it doesn't snow," said author and historian Mike Oriard. "There were schools in this era who thought it was more ethical to have the athletes sponsored by alumni providing jobs for young men. Somehow these young men would be tainted if they used institutional money."[10]

Led by the school presidents, the newly formed conference didn't waste time altering long-held traditions that would benefit the athletic programs of their members and the football teams specifically. In 1935, the SEC announced that it would be allowed within the conference for schools to provide student aid scholarships (tuition, books, board, and room) for all enrollees, including athletes. This decision created such an uproar in the press that Tulane president Wilber Smith felt the need to address the matter in his report to the National Collegiate Athletic

Association (NCAA) in 1936, saying, "This plan has now been in effect a year and I am convinced that it has elevated intercollegiate athletics to a higher plane, and in general has corrected the evils and problems which previously had made falsifiers out of many of the athletes."[11]

For the first time of many, the SEC set the precedent, and everyone else in collegiate athletics followed. By 1939, the NCAA initiated similar regulations for at-large membership regarding scholarships and grants-in-aid.

* * *

Alabama had been the premier college football program in the Southern Conference in the decade preceding the formation of the SEC. Challengers to the dominance of the Tide included Tulane, who finished without a loss in three consecutive seasons (1929–1931), culminating with an appearance in the Rose Bowl in 1931, and Tennessee under legendary head coach General Robert R. Neyland. But it was the Crimson Tide who immediately established themselves as the preeminent university of the fledgling SEC.

When Wallace Wade informed President Denny he would be leaving Tuscaloosa at the conclusion of the 1930 season, Denny solicited his input to help find his replacement. Wade suggested Frank Thomas, a former quarterback at Notre Dame who played for Knute Rockne and in 1930 was an assistant at rival Georgia. Commenting to Denny, Wade said that Thomas "would become one of the greatest coaches in the country. I don't believe you could pick a better man."[12] It would prove to be the ideal hire that would continue to build the legacy of success at Alabama.

Thomas would coach in Tuscaloosa for 16 years, win two national titles and four SEC championships and take Alabama to appearances in the Rose, Orange, and Cotton bowls. He brought to the South the wide-open offense he learned under Rockne in South Bend, the "Box Formation," leaning on speed, pre-snap shifting, and a relatively new weapon in college football, the forward pass, to move the ball down the field. As if it could be any other way, Alabama would win the very first SEC championship in football in the 1933 season with an unbeaten record in conference play. They followed that season with an SEC title, a Rose Bowl win, and a national championship in 1934. The team was led by Don Hutson, who was known as the Alabama Antelope. Hutson played for the Crimson Tide from 1932 to 1934 and followed his college playing days with an 11-year career in the National Football League (NFL). He was the first NFL player with 1,000 yards receiving in a season and led the Green Bay Packers to NFL championships in 1936, 1939, and 1944. Other standouts on those teams included All-American guard Tom Huke, quarterback Bill Lee, and an end named Paul W. Bryant: his friends called him "Bear."

While Alabama was occupied with laying the groundwork for what would be a century of prosperity on the gridiron, another school 300 miles to the northeast was establishing a winning tradition of their own. In the earliest days of college football in the state of Tennessee, the superior program resided in Nashville. A small, private school, Vanderbilt was home to one of the southern college football powers in the early 1900s. Twice scoring more than 100 points in a game and claiming national titles in 1921 and 1922, Vanderbilt dominated their rivalry with the University of Tennessee, winning 18 of the first 21 meetings. That all changed when 34-year-old Robert R. Neyland arrived in Knoxville. Told by the faculty chairman of athletics to "even the score with Vanderbilt; do something about our terrible standing in the series,"[13] the man with a military pedigree would end up doing more than ending Vanderbilt's run as the best college football program in the Volunteer State. From 1926 until he retired in 1952, Neyland would establish Tennessee as one of the powers of southern football.

When Neyland was hired to lead the Volunteer football program, he was an active member of the U.S. Army, serving as a captain. His head coaching career would twice be interrupted by service in the military: first in 1935 in Panama (he returned with the rank of major) and then missing the 1941–1945 seasons, serving as a general during World War II. Neyland wasted little time reversing the results in their rivalry with Vanderbilt. After losing his first matchup, 20–3, in 1926, Neyland would lose to his Nashville nemesis only three more times until retiring in 1952.

While it was Alabama that claimed the very first SEC title in 1933, it was Tennessee and Major Neyland that established the first dynasty in the conference. It took him a couple years to build the program after returning from Panama, but when he did, the Volunteers went on a dominating run, accomplishing a scoreless feat that has yet to be matched. Led by George "Bad News" Cafego, Ed Molinski, and Bob Suffridge, Tennessee went 10–0 in 1938, 1939, and 1940. Speaking about Cafego, Neyland remarked that he was a "practice bum. On the practice field he couldn't do anything right, but for two hours on a Saturday afternoon he did everything an All-American is supposed to do." He earned his nickname from an opponent who said he was bad news. He grew up poor in West Virginia and never knew his mother, and his father died when he was young. Playing football at Tennessee changed his life. "I had nothing. I didn't need a partial scholarship, I needed everything."[14] The 1939 Volunteers did not allow a single point to be scored against them in the regular season. They were crowned national champions in 1938 and 1940.

Speaking about Neyland, a former player said, "The general was not the easiest guy to work with Monday through Friday, but on Saturday he was a fatherly figure. On Saturday he was a warm man who gave you a lot of confidence."[15]

With the outbreak of World War II, Neyland was again called into military duty. He returned from the China–Burma–India front, this time with the rank of a general, to coach the 1946 season and instantly captured another SEC championship, his fourth. But following that season, he proved prophetic when he said, "It will take us five years to put Tennessee back on top."[16] In what would be his second-to-last season as head coach, Neyland guided Tennessee to another SEC title and their third national championship under his watch.

Neyland retired with a record of 173–31–12. Over the course of his tenure, he led the Vols to consecutive win streaks of 33, 28, and 23 games. In 1962, shortly after his death, the on-campus stadium was renamed in his honor. John Michaels, a guard on the 1951 national title team, said of his coach, "The general was always in complete control. He never got excited. He was highly organized and a great disciplinarian."[17]

* * *

For nearly 15 years, the Rose Bowl had been the only postseason college football event to gain any national traction. But in the mid-1930s, an enterprising businessman in New Orleans would add a southern jewel to the bowl game landscape.

In 1927, the publisher of the *New Orleans Item*, Colonel James M. Thomson, proposed the idea of a midwinter amateur college football showcase game. His sports editor, Fred Digby, came up with the name "Sugar Bowl" because the land where the proposed site of the game, Tulane Stadium, was located was a place where sugar had been crystallized in the past. The local community slowly warmed up to the idea, and in 1929, the mayor of New Orleans sent a delegation to propose the idea to the Southern Conference, asking the conference to approve and sanction the event. Their approval was denied, and the game was put on the back burner.

In early 1934, the proposition again began to gain steam when business, civic, and athletic organizations came together and created the Mid-Winter Sports Association with the specific purpose of creating the Sugar Bowl and hosting the event. By October 1934, the association announced it had an escrow in the sum of $30,000 to host and promote the game. The SEC was approached by the fledgling event with a proposal for an affiliation agreement, but the conference rejected the offer. On December 2 of that year, the association invited unbeaten (and local) Tulane and the only team in the North without a loss, Temple University, led by the famous "Pop" Warner. Tickets were available for $1.50 and $3.50. The public first met the announcement with trepidation but after considering the records of the teams snatched up tickets and made the inaugural Sugar Bowl a success, with more than 22,000 fans in attendance.

The Sugar Bowl quickly grew in popularity, and within two years, the association negotiated with Tulane University to add 14,000 seats by enclosing the north end zone of the stadium. But even that wasn't enough seats to quench the demand for tickets. In 1939, a citizens group was formed with the slogan "70,000 or bust" to enlarge the stadium once again, and the January 1, 1940, edition between Tulane and Texas A&M was played in front of 73,000 fans. By 1947, the president of the Sugar

Bowl had created a committee to study the feasibility of yet another expansion to Tulane Stadium. This resulted in an additional 13,000 seats, creating the largest double-decker stadium in the world.

A southern tradition had been born, and New Year's Day on Bourbon Street became the promised land for fans of the best team in the SEC. The Sugar Bowl would be coupled with the SEC for the next 80 years. In 1975, the game was moved indoors to the brand-new, state-of-the-art Louisiana Superdome. And in 1977, more than 40 years after initially considering the idea, the SEC and the Sugar Bowl became official partners, agreeing that the conference would send a team every year to represent the conference. Even without a formal association, an SEC team had appeared in all but four of the games prior to the 1977 Sugar Bowl. In the overall history of the Sugar Bowl, the game was played without an SEC team only seven times. In the 1990s, the college football postseason arrangements began to change, allowing certain bowl games to invite teams outside of their preferred partnership. From 1949 through 1998, only one game (1972, Oklahoma vs. Penn State) featured non-SEC teams. Alabama has the most appearances in the event, playing in the game 17 times. LSU, Georgia, Ole Miss, and Florida round out the top five.

* * *

In the 1930s and 1940s, as the SEC began to establish itself and its authority, the influence of the conference as a whole began to become larger than the institutions individually. With attendance during the lean years of the Great Depression at the forefront of many financial decisions, debate among universities regarding allowances for football games to be broadcast were fierce. The outlawing of this practice by the Southern Conference office was one of the many controversial items that led to the formation of the SEC. In 1934, just two seasons into existence, the new conference had found a sponsor (A. J. Norris Hill Company) for a "game of the week" radio broadcast. Instantly, the conference discovered that the broadcasts not only promoted SEC football to new fans but also did not diminish the gate receipts. They quickly reversed the ban on schools negotiating individual contracts for local broadcasts. It would not be the last time the SEC was out in front when it came to the power of media partnerships.

When the SEC was formed initially, a school president was designated as the commissioner. That changed in 1940, when former Mississippi governor Martin Sennett Conner was appointed to the position. He was given a salary of $7,500, which was covered by each school paying 1 percent of their gross football receipts.

Another change happened in 1940, the first of many membership adjustments for the SEC, when Sewanee announced they were leaving the conference. Sewanee school president Alexander Guerry showed his hand two years earlier, when he said in a speech to students, "A big time football policy for a college distorts the purpose of the college, destroys the sense of values and robs it of the opportunity to give its students a sense of values. Sewanee's prestige in Southern education and in the nation does not rest upon the football victories of the past, but upon the splendid academic and spiritual ideals which she has maintained."[18]

The small liberal arts school in Tennessee simply could not keep pace with their larger counterparts. The SEC, desiring to keep their membership numbers low, did not look for a replacement.

As the 1940s continued, so did the changes to the sport on the field and the administration of the sport off the field. The conference office moved to Birmingham, Alabama. The NCAA and the SEC disagreed over recruiting regulations. In 1939, Alabama played at Fordham, and the game was broadcast locally in New York City. Only a few hundred television sets existed at the time. It was the second sporting event carried on TV, with the Fordham game that took place the week before being the first. In 1951, the first televised game in the South took place on ABC. Appropriately, it featured Alabama facing the eventual national champions, Tennessee. The broadcast didn't hamper the attendance, as the game featured the largest home crowd of the season for the Tide. At the conclusion of World War II and again in 1956, the conference office recommended and attempted to create a balanced, round-robin schedule. Both times, nearly every school objected.

In 1936, the Associated Press (AP) began naming a national champion in college football each season, and while other organizations continue to do so, ending the season number one in the AP poll became the highest honor in the college football landscape. The SEC didn't capture this distinction until 1951 with General Neyland and his Tennessee Volunteers. Auburn won the AP crown in 1957 and LSU in 1958.

As the 1960s approached, more change was heading toward college football. The SEC was poised to continue to turn their passion for the sport into national success, and once again, it would fall on Alabama to carry the torch, led by an up-and-coming coach and his trademark houndstooth hat.

CHAPTER 2

A Foundation Forms

As COLLEGE FOOTBALL CHARGED INTO THE 1960S, GAINING IN POPU-larity both regionally and nationally, the foundational changes that occurred in the 1950s began to impact the membership of the SEC in ways that surprised even the most passionate observers. The debate among university administrators regarding the importance of athletics in general and the football program specifically had continued to heighten as interest in football increased among alumni and fans in the community.

The Ivy League officially formed in 1954, with member institutions agreeing to de-emphasize football. Spring practice was eliminated, athletic scholarships were not allowed, and teams were banned from competing in any postseason game. With this new vision in the Ivy League came a desire to recruit athletes who represented the student body at large. Schools like Yale and Princeton, so prominent in the early years of college football, would never again compete for national titles or appear in prestigious bowl games. On campuses where college football was still a focus, the pressure to win became even more pronounced as the popularity of the sport grew, causing costs to rise as programs competed against one another in areas off the field. Some of the more prominent programs from decades earlier stunningly decided to terminate their football programs. Two of the most noteworthy examples were Fordham University, a participant in the very first college football game to be broadcast on television, and Georgetown University, both of which shut down their programs in 1954.

The debates surrounding the priority that schools were placing on athletics extended into SEC territory by the early 1960s. The conference had been a leader in standardizing athletic scholarships in the 1930s, guiding the NCAA in writing policies for its institutions. But a disagreement over how those scholarships should be administered would lead to a charter member leaving the conference.

Georgia Tech has a proud football history. Legendary coach John Heisman led the program from 1904 through the 1919 season, and coach Bill Alexander followed that up in 1928 with their first 10-win season and Rose Bowl victory. In 1931, a former all-American quarterback who played for General Neyland at Tennessee changed the fortunes of Georgia Tech football forever when he spurned his alma mater to accept an assistant coaching position in Atlanta for the Yellow Jackets. Bobby Dodd began his illustrious career at Tech under Alexander and never left the school. He assumed head coaching duties in 1945 and by 1950 had brought Tech back into the national spotlight.

Under Alexander, the Yellow Jackets had played in the Orange, Sugar, and Cotton bowls in the early 1940s and had claimed shares of the conference title but had yet to break through on a national level. Dodd picked up where Alexander left off, leading Tech to the Orange Bowl in 1947, where his unconventional coaching style took center stage. "As soon as we get to Miami, we assembled at the hotel, and he took us to the beach to go swimming. We beat Kansas [in the game] and everyone was happy," said Red Patton, a Tech player from 1947 to 1950. College Football Hall of Famer and former Yellow Jacket Ray Beck, who played from 1949 to 1951, said, "Coach Dodd believed that you should never leave your best effort out on the practice field."[1] Dodd wanted practices to be light and fun, the very opposite mindset of his college coach, Robert Neyland.

The 1951 and 1952 Georgia Tech teams were two of the best in school history. Undefeated both years, the Yellow Jackets won back-to-back SEC championships (the first to do so in the conference since Tennessee in 1938–1940) and shares of the national title both years. In 1956, Tech was again awarded the national championship by three voting committees. But as college football continued to gain in prominence and the pressure mounted at each university to win games, the conference rules relating to scholarships came to a head for Dodd in the early 1960s.

Per SEC bylaws at the time, each school was permitted to award 140 scholarships for football and men's basketball: the "140 rule," as it was known within conference circles. But football programs were also allowed, under conference rules, to sign up to 45 new recruits each year. And this drove Bobby Dodd crazy. He felt that once a school committed to a player, the school should stay committed and invest in the player, even if he didn't live up to his potential on the field. But Dodd also suspected that that was not what rival coaches and schools in the SEC were doing. Dodd began complaining publicly that his conference opponents would over-sign players each year and then remove players from the team who were not performing on the field.

Taz Anderson, a captain for Georgia Tech, said, "Coach Dodd would not run you off if you met the part he required. If you went to class and did the work, he'd get you a degree." Bill Curry, a player for Dodd and later a head coach in the SEC at Kentucky and Alabama, said, "[Sticking with players] was an obsession with coach Dodd. I didn't play very much my first two seasons. I was one of those he could have run off."[2]

By clinging to his principles, Dodd recruited only about 35 players each year, giving his rivals approximately 10 more recruits each season. In 1962, Dodd was passionate enough about the 140 rule that he convinced school president Edwin Harrison to abolish it by vote at the annual SEC meetings. But the vote failed. It was brought before the conference again in January 1963. But even with the backing of the SEC commissioner, the vote failed once more. Dodd went back to work gathering the necessary votes to finally get the rule removed, and by the summer of 1963, he felt he would get his way. But in July of that year, an article came out in the *Atlanta Journal-Constitution* claiming, "Georgia Tech to Quit SEC Next January."[3] More and more people, both those at schools inside the conference and observers in the press, were beginning to question if Dodd was simply using the 140 rule to get out of the SEC and become an independent, with the ability to build a schedule as they saw fit and to keep all the money they earned to themselves.

At the annual meetings in late January 1964, the issue would finally come to a head. Over the course of the three-day meetings, newspaper articles speculated on the outcome, seemingly going back and forth on both whether the rule would be dropped and what the consequences would be if it were or were not abolished. At the end of the second day of meetings, the *Birmingham News* quoted Alabama president Frank Rose saying, "I think we are going to have a compromise that will keep Georgia Tech with us. We are trying to work it out. I don't think anyone wants Tech to leave the Southeastern Conference."[4] But the second day ended with the coaches and athletic directors voting to keep the 140 rule in place. It would be up to the presidents on the final day of meetings to solidify the decision. But before a vote could be taken, Harrison addressed his colleagues. "Georgia Tech's interest is best served by withdrawal from the conference, effective June 30, 1964."

The 140 rule was staying. Georgia Tech was leaving. It was an announcement that, at the time, was stunning, but as the years passed, the unintended consequences of leaving the SEC would become nearly impossible to quantify.

From the inaugural SEC season in 1933 until Tech left the conference following the 1963 season, they had a record of 206–110–12. During that period, they won five conference titles and claimed a share of three national championships. They played in 15 bowl games, including nine in the 12 years previous to leaving the SEC. In the 20 seasons following their defection, Georgia Tech would compete as an independent, relegated to wandering on the periphery of the college football landscape. From 1964 until they joined the Atlantic Coast Conference (ACC) in 1983, Georgia Tech football did not come close to approaching their previous success. With no conference championship to chase each season, they went 104–100–5, appeared in six bowl games, and did not compete for a national title.

Bobby Dodd coached through the end of the 1966 season, with his final game on the sidelines in the Orange Bowl on January 1, 1967. He remained as the Georgia Tech athletic director until 1976 and stayed on at the school as a consultant until his death in 1988. He remains a legend at Tech, with the on-campus football stadium bearing his name to this day.

In an article announcing the decision, the *New York Times* commented, "Tech stands to make a considerable gain financially by its withdrawal from the conference. Under SEC regulations, Georgia Tech had to share with other conference members its proceeds from its numerous postseason bowl games and television appearances. The school has participated in a dozen bowl games and made a similar number of television appearances since the end of World War II. Robert Eskew, the athletic business manager, estimated that Georgia Tech will gain about $100,000 over past revenue on all future television appearances and from $25,000 to $50,000 more on all future bowl games."[5]

But in the years that followed, as the SEC continued to rise in national influence and prominence, Tech fans and alumni were left to wonder what might have been had they navigated their frustrations differently and remained a member of the SEC.

The SEC was chartered with 13 member institutions, and after Georgia Tech withdrew, the conference was down to 11, but another school was on their way out, and this time it wasn't near as big a surprise as a national power like Tech leaving.

In the 1930s, Tulane was a dominant force in the SEC. An undefeated season and Sugar Bowl win in the second year of the conference's existence punctuated the place Tulane occupied in the pecking order of the SEC elites. But a major internal institutional switch in philosophy in the 1950s changed Tulane football forever.

From the inception of the conference in 1933 through the 1950 season, Tulane football captured three SEC titles, which is as many as fellow charter members Kentucky (two titles), Mississippi State (one), and Vanderbilt (zero) have combined. They participated in three bowl games and had a winning record in 14 of those seasons. Playing at Tulane Stadium, home of the Sugar Bowl, Green Wave football was an event in New Orleans. The 1949 team that won the SEC championship averaged more than 37,000 fans per game, leading the conference in attendance. Tulane football was such an event that it was partially responsible for the now revered tradition of night games up the highway in Baton Rouge. LSU administrators were looking for ways to draw more fans to their games and moved their kickoffs to 8:00 p.m. to avoid competition with Tulane home games that began in the early afternoon. The hope was that football fans living in New Orleans could attend both a Tulane game and an LSU game on the same Saturday.

But everything began to change in 1951. Tulane president Rufus Harris, long in favor of scaling back intercollegiate athletics to underscore the importance of academics, cut the number of football scholarships available at the university from 100 to 75 and the travel roster down to 38 players.[6] Salaries of the coaching staff were reduced, recruiting travel was limited, and players no longer could study physical education with no academic major. They had to be on track to earn a bachelor's degree in a specific field of study.

The de-emphasis on football had an immediate impact on the success of the Tulane program. Following the initial campaign with fewer scholarships, head coach Henry Frnka resigned. A road trip to Atlanta to face Georgia Tech resulted in a reporter checking the hotel registry to see if, in fact, Tulane was actually attempting to field a team with only 38 players, which indeed was what was discovered. Over the next 10 seasons, two more coaches would come and go, and the Green Wave won only 14 SEC games and never finished above .500. By the early 1960s, whispers began to creep into conference circles that Tulane was going to either leave the SEC or be removed by the other member institutions. From 1961 through the 1964 season, Tulane had a conference record of 2–23–1.

On December 31, 1964, Tulane president Herbert Longenecker (also serving at the time as the SEC's vice president) announced the school would be leaving the conference they helped charter at the conclusion of the 1965–1966 school year, two years after Georgia Tech moved on. Head coach Tommy O'Boyle didn't seem concerned at the time, saying, "It sure can't do us any harm. Tulane is a national university. Now we can play a national schedule."[7]

Longenecker also claimed that a major reason for the withdrawal was to play a national schedule, saying at the time, "Tulane University has changed in the past two decades from an institution, drawing its students mostly from the area to one attracting students from all states of the nation. The purposes of the university, for this reason, will be better served by scheduling intersectional games. We also wish to have freedom to design schedules that will improve our competitive position and avoid the overload situation Tulane has experienced in recent years."[8]

Tulane football would never be the same again. And the SEC, now down three members from its original group of 13 institutions, would move forward into the late 1960s, a time of political turmoil and civil unrest in the United States, with 10 solid schools ready to build the foundation for a conference that could dominate college football in the years to come.

* * *

The years following World War II were full of ups and downs for the original premier program in the SEC. Alabama had a winning record each season from 1946 until 1951, but they ended up in the middle of the pack most of those years, earning just one bowl bid. In 1952, the Tide finished below .500 but bounced back to win their first SEC championship in seven years in 1953. Following that title run, Alabama endured the worst stretch in school history, going 4–24–2 from 1955 to 1957, including a winless season in 1956. To make matters worse, in 1957, archrival Auburn obliterated the Tide, 40–0, and won the national championship. Alabama football was at an unthinkable low point. They turned to one of their own to reconstruct the program.

Paul Bryant was born in 1913 in Moro Bottom, Arkansas. He had 12 siblings, and at times, his mode of transportation to school was a mule. As a 13-year-old, he played in his first football game, with cleats screwed into the only pair of shoes he owned, forcing him to wear the cleats everywhere he went for weeks thereafter. When he was 14 years old, he volunteered to wrestle a bear at a local carnival, with the prize being a $1 bill. "There was a poster out front with a picture of a bear, and a guy was offering a dollar a minute to anyone who would wrestle the bear. The guy who was supposed to wrestle the bear didn't show up, so they egged me on. They let me and my friends into the picture show free, and I wrestled this scrawny bear to the floor. I went around later to get my money, but the guy with the bear had flown the coop. All I got out of the whole thing was a nickname."[9] "Bear" Bryant was born.

Bryant, growing into a solid six-foot, four-inch frame, played on the state championship team at Fordyce High School but left for the University of Alabama before getting his diploma. The following fall, he practiced with the Tide while taking classes at a Tuscaloosa high school to become eligible to play in college. He was a member of the 1934 national championship team and became known as the "other end" playing opposite Don Hutson, a future member of the Pro Football Hall of Fame.

During the 1935 season, the fame of that "other end" began to grow as Bryant found himself leading the Tide to victory against rival Tennessee with a broken leg that he had suffered in the previous game. Ironically, his participation in the game had not been planned. Years later, he recounted the pregame speech given by assistant coach Hank Crisp, who told the team in the locker room, "I'll tell you gentlemen one thing. I don't know about the rest of you. I don't know what you're going to do. But I know one damn thing. Old 34 will be after 'em, he'll be after their asses." Bryant continued, "In those days they changed the players' numbers almost every week to help sell programs. So [coach] is up there talking about old 34 and I look down, and I'm 34! I had no idea of playing."[10]

Bryant was selected in the fourth round of the very first NFL draft held in 1936. But after graduation, he decided to stay at Alabama as an assistant coach. His mother had wanted him to become a minister. "I told her that coaching and preaching were a lot alike, but I don't think she believed me," Bryant said years later.[11] He stayed at his alma mater for four years before moving on to Vanderbilt to become the lead assistant coach. In the 1940 season, Bear Bryant found himself as the head coach for the very first time when the actual Vanderbilt head coach was too ill to attend the game. Bryant presided over a 7–7 tie, and as he recounted in his autobiography, he was not pleased with his efforts.

"The night before the game I went out into the country and puked my guts out. My big chance. All I really had to do was give them that lineup. Instead I coached a 7–0 victory into a 7–7 tie. Kentucky didn't have a great team. We struggled along and finally went ahead in the first half when our tailback passed for a touchdown."[12] While disappointed in himself, he told the local paper after the game what he thought of his players. "I couldn't ask a bunch of boys to play a better game than they did today. All of them gave a wonderful exhibition. It's too bad they didn't win after rising to such great heights. I'm thoroughly satisfied with their play. We were in the worst physical condition we have been in all season and I am still wondering how some of them stayed in there as well as they did. These boys certainly are fighters and they've got plenty of guts."[13]

After only two seasons in Nashville, Bryant interviewed for the head coaching position at his home-state University of Arkansas. But fate intervened, and he never got the chance to accept the position. While driving back to Vanderbilt, Bryant heard the news of the attack on Pearl Harbor. He immediately joined the U.S. Navy and served until the end of the war.

On returning to football, he was named the head coach at the University of Maryland in 1945. But after disagreements with the administration, he departed only a year later. His next stop was the University of Kentucky, where he was named head coach at the basketball-crazed school. The Wildcats had never finished with a record above .500 in SEC play before Bryant arrived. It took him a couple of years to build the program, but the future hall of fame coach led Kentucky to its greatest run in school history. Their very first bowl appearance occurred in 1949, and that was followed by an 11–1 season in 1950, an SEC title, a final AP ranking of number seven, and an astonishing upset of top-ranked Oklahoma in the Sugar Bowl. But by 1953, Bryant was becoming increasingly frustrated with the lack of attention the administration was giving to the football program, believing that nothing he could ever do would help place the sport on equal ground with basketball. He clashed with legendary hoops coach Adolph Rupp, saying years later, "The trouble was that we were too much alike. He wanted basketball to be No. 1, and I wanted football No. 1. In an environment like that, one or the other has to go."[14]

Bryant accepted the head coaching position at Texas A&M in 1954, and Kentucky football has yet to reach the same heights as when the "Bear" was prowling their sidelines. During his tenure in Lexington, Bryant marshaled Kentucky to Sugar, Orange, and Cotton bowl appearances and five top 20 finishes in the AP poll. Over the next 70 years combined, the Wildcats would finish in the top 20 only five times. The 1950 SEC championship remains the only outright title Kentucky has ever won in the conference.

Taking over a struggling program in College Station, Bryant would work similar magic with the Texas A&M program as he had at his previous stops. His first squad suffered through a 1–9 season in 1954, but by the second year, the Aggies were rolling, finishing with a 7–2–1 record. The year 1956 would prove to be a banner one for Texas A&M football. They ended the season unbeaten, won the Southwest Conference (SWC) title for the first time in nearly 20 years, halted a four-game losing streak against rival Texas, and finished ranked number five in the final AP poll. While the 1957 season stopped short of a conference championship, the Aggies earned an appearance in the Gator Bowl and a final AP ranking in the top 10.

But with Alabama in the throes of their worst stretch in school history, they turned to their former player and assistant coach to bring the Crimson Tide back to their rightful perch at the top of the SEC.

Bryant began meeting in secret with Alabama officials with about a month left in the 1957 season. Even though he had seven years remaining on his contract with Texas A&M, the pull to rebuild Alabama was too strong. "I left because my school called me. Mama called," he said. "And when mama calls, you just have to come running."[15] He agreed to a 10-year contract worth $17,000 annually and a new house, and he immediately got to work changing the culture of the program. Lineman Dave Singleton said the new coach made his vision very clear in the first meeting with the team. "I'm not worried about whether I'm going to win or lose," Bryant proclaimed to the team. "I know I'm going to win. I know that. And I'm not worried about my assistant coaches. I know they're winners. And I'm not worried about whether Alabama is going to win. I know that. The only thing I don't know is how many of you in this room are winners, and how many of you will be with us."[16]

It didn't take long for Bear Bryant to deliver every one of those declarations he made to his players when he first arrived. Two seasons into his tenure, he had Alabama back in the postseason, as the Tide played Penn

State in the Liberty Bowl. It had been five years between bowl appearances for Alabama, and the school would never have a postseason drought that long again. The 1961 season represented Bryant's fourth year at the helm and was the pinnacle of his rebuilding process at Alabama. After a convincing victory on national television over rival Tennessee in the fifth game of the year, he revealed to his players his true feelings about their potential. "After that game he came on the bus and told us we had a great football team. Three or four weeks before that he had told us we wouldn't win a game, that we were sorry as hell," all-American and future College Football Hall of Fame member Billy Neighbors said.[17]

Once again, Bryant was right about his team. The 1961 Alabama squad went undefeated, ending the season with a win over Arkansas for their first ever Sugar Bowl victory. They would bring home an SEC championship, a distinction that had not happened in nearly 10 years for the program, and earn the national title from the AP for the first time ever, only the second SEC team to do so (Tennessee in 1951 was the first). Alabama had not claimed a share of the national championship since 1945, more than 15 years earlier. In four short years, Paul "Bear" Bryant not only had returned Alabama football to the apex of the SEC but also was setting up a 20-year run that would leave every other school in the South in their wake.

* * *

From the earliest years of the SEC, scheduling among conference members had always been an imprecise adventure. Travel considerations, win probability, long-held grudges, and more were the ingredients coaches would use to concoct their annual schedule. And as much as the conference office attempted to create uniformity across the conference, the coaches, in particular the powerful coaches who won the majority of their games, pushed back. It would be more than 50 years into the existence of the SEC before true consistency was established.

In 1933, the first year of the SEC, the 13 members of the conference played a varying amount of conference games. Conference champion Alabama played six games. LSU finished second but played only five games. Finishing 3–1, third-place Georgia played in four conference games. Tennessee won five games that year, the same number as the SEC champion, but played a total of seven games. The following year was just as baffling. Both Tulane and Alabama went unbeaten in conference play, but the Green Wave won the championship because they played eight games and Alabama seven. Five more times in the next 10 years, the SEC would have teams at the top of the conference with the same number of losses but a differing number of wins.

At the end of World War II, the conference office, led by commissioner Martin Conner, proposed a number of changes to further the mission of the SEC, including recruiting rules, compensation for conference employees, an association of officials, and a balanced schedule. Everything was adopted with the exception of the schedule proposal. In 1952, the conference office was finally able to establish a rule requiring each school to play at least six conference games. Again in 1956, the conference attempted to ratify a balanced, round-robin schedule, but it was soundly rejected by the member schools.

Adding to the confusion, between 1954 and 1968, 16 games were played by SEC teams against schools not in the conference that counted as conference games in the standings. The dilemma began in 1954, when Ole Miss ran into scheduling difficulties and was unable to find a sixth SEC team that would play them. Prior to the season, the SEC designated their game against SWC powerhouse Arkansas as a conference game. The Rebels won the conference in 1954 with only one "SEC" loss: at home to Arkansas.

By the late 1960s, the conference gained agreement from member schools to have two permanent rivals each year and a rotation of games against other teams in the conference. But with coaches retaining the flexibility to build the majority of the schedule, abnormalities remained, and win probability persisted as the driving factor in who played who and where the game took place.

Ole Miss and Auburn played each other only twice in the first 20 years of SEC football, even though the campuses were less than 300 miles apart. A three-game series ensued in the early 1950s but ended after an upset victory by the Tigers in 1953. After the stunning defeat, legendary Ole Miss coach John Vaught stood in front of his team on the bus as they awaited departure back to Oxford and angrily declared, "Boys, get a good look. No Ole Miss team will ever come here again."[18] It would be 20 years before they ventured to the plains of Auburn again, three years after Vaught retired. The only SEC school closer to the Ole Miss campus than Auburn, other than Mississippi State, their in-state rival down the road in Starkville, was Alabama. But that series also went on a 20-year hiatus, with no Alabama–Ole Miss contest taking place between 1944 and 1965. For much of that time, they were the two powers in the conference, and speculation holds that the two coaches had a gentleman's agreement to not play each other. Robert Khayat, who played for Ole Miss from 1957 to 1959 and became the school's chancellor in 1995, said, "We were always told that Alabama wouldn't play us. Later, I found out, the Alabama players were told it was because we refused to play them."[19]

Georgia and Tennessee, separated by only 235 miles and the Great Smoky Mountains, went 31 years without playing each other. Before the 1968 season, these two charter members had met only twice as SEC foes (1936 and 1937). Both games were massive Tennessee wins, with the Volunteers not allowing Georgia to score a point in either contest, with scores of 46–0 in 1936 and 32–0 in 1937. Starting in 1968, they played four games in five years but then took another long hiatus, forcing the conference office to step in and order the two schools to face off in the 1980 season. When the schools got back to the conference and said they were unable to come to an agreement on when and where to play, SEC commissioner Boyd McWhorter called Vanderbilt athletic director Roy Kramer.

"We're putting together a brand new scheduling committee, and we'd like you to be on it," McWhorter told him. Kramer said he would be happy to help in any way that he could, but after not hearing back from the office on what his duties were or even when the committee would be meeting, he reached back out to McWhorter. "Roy, *you're* the committee," McWhorter said. "We have an issue between Georgia and Tennessee, you're brand new and kind of neutral in all this, I'll let you talk to them and work it out." The only date that worked was opening weekend, so that is when they met, with Georgia winning both games in

1980 and 1981. It would be another decade before they would begin an annual rivalry.[20]

In their 30 years in the SEC, Georgia Tech played Mississippi State only twice and faced Ole Miss once, and that was in a bowl game. Georgia and LSU, on opposite ends of the geography of the SEC, didn't have a single matchup from 1953 through 1978. LSU and Auburn did not play a game against each other from 1942 until 1970. Former Auburn athletic director David Housel said, "There just wasn't any natural reason to play LSU. They just weren't anywhere around. They were part of the conference, but they weren't part of our conference."[21]

Even after the mandate from the conference office requiring schools to play a minimum of six games, LSU won the conference in 1970 with a 5–0 record. Tennessee finished in second place with a 4–1 mark, while Auburn went 5–2 and was third place in the standings. By 1971, schools began to adhere to the six-game directive, and no team would again play fewer than the requisite amount. The SEC office did put into place an allowance for teams to play more than six conference games—but only if the schools went through the conference to schedule the additional contest. This being the SEC, that rule was ignored in some cases. In 1980 and 1981, Alabama scheduled a series with Ole Miss, but because they circumvented the conference in doing so, those games were not counted in the standings. Alabama and Georgia finished with identical 6–0 SEC records in 1981, tying for the championship. Had Bear Bryant gone through the conference to schedule the series with the Rebels, they would have claimed the conference title with a 7–0 SEC record.

* * *

Nate Northington was an exceptional football player at Thomas Jefferson High School in Louisville, Kentucky, in 1965. In today's college football landscape, he would receive scholarship offers from schools all over the South. But in the mid-1960s, he had few options to continue to play the sport he loved at the next level. Nate Northington was African American. As the country grappled with the historical injustices done to African Americans and the civil rights movement was pushing forward and making gains in the 1950s, the South held tightly to their segregationist beliefs. And nowhere was that more apparent than in southern college football stadiums.

By the time Northington was wrapping up his senior season of high school football, change was beginning to materialize, ever so slowly, in colleges across the South. The landmark U.S. Supreme Court ruling of *Brown v. Board of Education* in 1954 brought integration to classrooms at all levels of schools. As the northernmost university in the SEC, Kentucky inevitably—and perhaps at times unwillingly—broke racial barriers. In 1948, Lyman T. Johnson filed suit to gain admission to Kentucky and enrolled with nearly 30 other black students at the university in the fall of 1949, with all classes becoming desegrated with the 1954 ruling. Other campuses in the SEC would experience a much longer timeline.

In the fall of 1962, the University of Mississippi was still not integrated. James Meredith had brought a suit against the university two years earlier claiming that he was denied entry based on his race. Even though he lost his first case, the U.S. Court of Appeals overturned the decision in June 1962 and required Mississippi to admit Meredith that fall. Leading up to the first day of classes on September 30, the university president took the field at halftime of a home football game to declare his opposition to the ruling. Riots broke out, forcing Meredith to spend the night under federal protection. He eventually became the first black graduate of the University of Mississippi in August 1963.

African American athletes had begun to make inroads and find opportunities to play on campuses in the North and the West years earlier. Before breaking the color barrier in Major League Baseball in 1947, Jackie Robinson was part of the first all-black backfield at the University of California, Los Angeles (UCLA), in the early 1940s. In 1960, Minnesota won the national championship led by black quarterback Sandy Stephens, who helped the Gophers capture a Rose Bowl win and earned most-valuable-player honors of the historic game along the way. Star Syracuse running back Ernie Davis won the Heisman Trophy in 1961, becoming the first African American to earn college football's top individual honor. Michigan State won the national championship in 1965 while fielding a team with 23 black players, including 10 starters. Thirty-three million people watched the Spartans play to a 10–10 tie against Notre Dame in 1966 on television, which was more than the viewership for the first-ever Super Bowl a month later.

Change was happening in every other part of the country. But the South was still clinging desperately to the way things had always been. In 1962, the University of Maryland fielded their first African American player, Darryl Hill. The pushback was immediate, even if the ultimatums were, in the end, empty. Fellow ACC members South Carolina and Clemson threatened to leave the conference but remained and played their scheduled games against the Terrapins, where Hill had to endure racist taunts from the opposing fans. In 1966, Southern Methodist University (SMU) in the SWC integrated the Texas-centric conference with Jerry LeVias, who developed into a star wide receiver. Two years later, LeVias would travel with his Mustang teammates to Alabama to play on the campus of Auburn University and score what is believed to be the first touchdown in an SEC stadium by a black player. It was only five months after Dr. Martin Luther King Jr. had been assassinated. Years later, LeVias would say, "People today do not realize the price and pain that was paid by an individual that broke barriers in segregation."[22]

By 1963, administrators at the University of Kentucky were beginning to have concerns that they would lose funding unless they integrated their athletic program. New school president John W. Oswald and Kentucky governor Ned Breathitt encouraged head football coach Charlie Bradshaw to identify potential individuals who could become the first black football players at the school. By the time Northington was invited to the governor's mansion in December 1965 at the conclusion of his final high school football season, he was close to accepting a scholarship from Purdue in the northern state of Indiana. "It was a tough situation, [thinking of] going into Mississippi and Alabama to play [road games]. The deciding factor was when Governor Breathitt invited me and my family to the Governor's Mansion. He reassured me he would do everything to protect me."[23] After contemplating the words of the governor, he remembers thinking, "Integrating the athletic programs in the SEC would remove one of the last vestiges of segregation in the South and move the country forward."[24] On December 19, 1965, Northington signed with Kentucky and helped change the SEC forever.

Lineman Greg Page also signed with Kentucky that winter, and together with Northington, they would become the first black football players on scholarship in the SEC. In a terribly unfortunate accident in fall camp as a sophomore, Page injured his spine and died 38 days later. On September 30, 1967, the day following the death of his roommate and best friend, Northington played in Kentucky's first conference game of the season as the Wildcats hosted Mississippi. With a heavy heart and grief that he had only begun to comprehend, Northington would play three minutes before hurting his shoulder and leaving the game. But history had been made and a trail blazed. An African American had played for an SEC team against a fellow conference foe.

Northington would finish out the season playing for Kentucky, including facing Auburn on the road in Alabama and enduring racist taunts directed at him from the bleachers. He had missed classes visiting Page in the hospital after the injury, and the emotional toll of losing his best friend eventually forced Northington to move on from Kentucky. After the season ended, he transferred to Western Kentucky, where he finished out his football career as a star running back, including helping the team win their conference in 1970.

With the pioneering efforts of Northington and Page, the SEC was integrated, the final major conference to do so. Other schools began to follow suit, but the luminary of the conference, the University of Alabama football team, was still competing with white players only. Progress was slow, but it was also persistent. In 1969, Wilber Hackett, a linebacker at Kentucky, became the first African American to be named captain of an SEC team in any sport. That same season, Auburn integrated its team with James Owens, a running back from Fairfield, Alabama. As the lone African American football player on the roster in the state that was at the heart of the civil rights movement, it was a foreboding opportunity for Owens. He was refused service at barbershops and restaurants when with his teammates and heard racial epithets directed toward him on and off the field.

"The first three years that I was [at Auburn], there were days I got up and said, this is the day, I'm going home. It's not worth it." Owens recalled years later. "And I would call my mom and say 'I'm coming home.' And she'd say, 'No. Stay.'"[25] In 2012, Auburn established the James Owens Courage Award, given annually to an Auburn football player who has demonstrated courage in the face of adversity.

By 1970, half the conference varsity squads were integrated, with Tennessee, Florida, and Mississippi State joining Kentucky and Auburn. That same season, Alabama hosted USC in a showdown where the result would become a congested mix of myth and reality. USC featured an all-black backfield, including Clarence Davis, who hailed from Birmingham. The Trojans ran all over Alabama, stomping the Tide, 42–21, in a game that was never in doubt. As the years passed, legends arose that this was the moment Bear Bryant finally decided to recruit black players. But that wasn't the first humiliating defeat the Tide had suffered at the hands of an integrated team. Rival Tennessee, with three black players, had throttled Alabama a year earlier in Birmingham, 41–14. Wilbur Jackson, an African American from Ozark, Alabama, was already on scholarship for Bryant and playing on the freshman team (freshmen were ineligible to compete in NCAA athletics at that time) in 1970.

Jackson would shine over the next three years as a star running back and go on to a stellar NFL career, including winning the Super Bowl while playing for Washington in 1983. The decision to attend school at Alabama, where only a few years earlier the governor tried to stop integration of the state's flagship university by literally standing in the doorway of a building on campus, wasn't an easy one for Jackson. "As it got closer, it got a little bit scary. But people were fair to me. The thing that really got me was coach Bryant telling me on my recruiting trip 'If you ever have a problem, you come see me.' The entire time I was there, I never needed to go see coach Bryant."[26]

The progress would continue to move forward for African American football players in the SEC. In 1972, Condredge Holloway became the first black quarterback in conference history to start for his team. As the signal caller for Tennessee, Holloway would guide the Vols to a 25–9–2 record and a bowl appearance in each of his three seasons. All 10 SEC schools became integrated by the start of the 1972 season, with LSU, Georgia, Mississippi, and Vanderbilt joining Alabama. While it would still be years before rosters would be filled with black players, the energy of the movement, combined with the courage of the young men who initially broke barriers at individual schools, would not be stopped.

Paul Karem, a quarterback for Kentucky in the late 1960s, said, "Government programs didn't break down the barriers of race in the South. Neither did busing. Military intervention didn't do it and social engineering didn't do it. As much as anything or anybody, football did it."[27]

* * *

As time marched on, so did the momentum of the SEC. But while the success on the field was picking up the pace, a major development was festering behind the scenes in college athletic departments all over the country. Rights fees for sports properties to be broadcast on millions of TV sets all across the country were escalating, and the NCAA had kept their member institutions under lock and key for nearly three decades. By the early 1980s, the University of Georgia was about to lead the charge to change college football on TV forever.

CHAPTER 3

The NCAA

Never Compromise Anything Anytime

IN THE AFTERMATH OF WORLD WAR II, THE UNITED STATES WAS A rapidly changing country, and innovations in technology were leading the revolution. In the 1930s and 1940s, television sets had been a novelty, something only the very affluent could afford to place in their living rooms. But by 1950, TV had become more than a curious medium for the ultrarich. In a matter of only three years, from 1947 to 1950, the number of television sets in use exploded from 7,000 to 9.2 million. With national companies such as CBS, NBC, and ABC working to establish a presence and local stations popping up by the hundreds all over the country, airtime schedules that needed programming were plentiful, and competition among broadcasters was fierce. Sports properties, including college football, were identified immediately by network executives and advertising agencies as must-see TV.

The Army–Navy game in 1945 represented the very first network broadcast of a college football game, as NBC aired the game on three affiliate stations in New York City, Philadelphia, and Schenectady, New York. In the late 1940s, schools located in areas with enough television sets arranged contracts with local stations to have home games broadcast to the local community, including Georgia Tech, Oklahoma, and USC. But national power Notre Dame and Ivy League member Penn recognized that the fledgling medium could build their brand and fill their coffers. Just as the school had done in the 1920s under legendary coach

Knute Rockne, when they were barnstorming trailblazers, Notre Dame led the way with TV. In 1950, the small private school signed a contract with the DuMont network to have all their home games broadcast nationally for a rights fee of $185,000. Penn followed suit, inking a deal with ABC for $150,000.

While a few universities and athletic departments saw TV as a way to bring greater exposure to their football programs and build interest in their teams, most others viewed it as a monumental threat. Revenue received from attendance at home football games provided much of the necessary funds for each athletic department to operate. If the games are shown on television, who is going to buy tickets? From the executives at the NCAA to the administrators at conference offices to the university presidents and football coaches on campuses across the country, college football games on TV became a sector they were determined to legislate and control.

In 1950, the same year Notre Dame and Penn were embracing TV, the Big Ten passed a resolution forbidding conference members to broadcast football games. The SEC attempted to pass a similar measure, but Georgia Tech went against the wishes of the conference office and allowed games to be seen on TV. The Pacific Coast Conference members had a total of 30 games on TV in 1950. But attendance was falling, and the blame fell directly on the shoulders of television.

In January of 1951, the member schools of the NCAA gathered in Dallas for their annual convention. Thomas Hamilton, the University of Pittsburgh athletic director at the time, recalled the scene years later. "You have to understand that we were dealing with a very dire situation. We were fighting for the future of the sport. There was almost a sense of panic about the whole process."[1]

Ticket sales in college football nationwide were down 6 percent but had fallen precipitously in local areas where games were shown on TV. UCLA reported a 26 percent decline in attendance in 1950. Schools in New England claimed a combined drop of 29 percent. Schools and conferences felt they had to put a stop to the disruption to the sport before it was destroyed forever.

At the convention, SEC commissioner Bernie Moore left no doubt where the conference stood on the matter. "It is the near-unanimous opinion of the Southeastern Conference that a definite television policy should be established by the NCAA. If direct telecasts of Southeastern Conference games are permitted, such a procedure would almost ruin football in our area."[2]

Rather than join Notre Dame and Penn in using a free market to secure their own national television agreements, the NCAA member schools wanted central control. "We had to act to keep Notre Dame and Penn from being on every week. That could have been so damaging to college football," said Jeff Coleman, athletic business manager at Alabama.[3]

It was put to a member vote, but the outcome was never in question. By a margin of 161–7, the NCAA was given jurisdiction by its members to control all broadcasts in 1951. All schools were forbidden from attempting to sign separate contracts outside of the approval of the NCAA.

Penn was devastated by the result but resolute in continuing to forge their own path with TV. Frannie Murray, the athletic director for the Quakers, said at the time, "I think we are being a little shortsighted when we look at a crowded stadium and think that is the saturation point." University president Harold Stassen issued a statement blasting the NCAA, saying, "Central control is a kind of disease which slips into the minds of men around the world. But it is not the American approach to problems."[4]

Convinced that the NCAA overstepped their authority, Penn shrugged off the newly passed regulation and negotiated a one-year deal with ABC for $180,000 to broadcast all home games in 1951. The reaction from the governing body and its members was swift. Penn was labeled a "member not in good standing" with the NCAA. Four schools set to face the Quakers in the 1951 season, Cornell, Columbia, Dartmouth, and Princeton, threatened to cancel their games with Penn if they chose to go through with the plan, even though Penn had promised to split the revenue from ABC with their opponent. Penn was faced with the dilemma of going through with their signed contract to broadcast all home games and possibly ending up with cancellations, going to court to stop the NCAA from restricting their TV rights, or dropping the issue entirely and falling in line with the majority. After unsuccessfully recruiting Notre Dame to join them in the fight, Penn ultimately relented. The contract was called off.

With the rebel cause behind them, the NCAA again proposed legislation to its members at the annual convention the following year. In January 1952, by a vote of 163–8, the NCAA was given power to create a television committee with the authority to construct a national TV series and to negotiate with the networks. On June 6, 1952, NBC agreed to pay $1.14 million for the rights to broadcast college football games. Aspects of the contract included the ability for games to be telecast on 11 different Saturdays over the course of the season, and, perhaps most significant, no team could appear more than once per season. Driven by angst over losing fans in the stands to fans on couches, the members of the NCAA had achieved their objective of keeping TV a minor part of college football. It would be nearly 30 years before another school would dare challenge the muscular supremacy of the NCAA as it related to broadcast rights.

The 1950s represented the coming-of-age for television. Iconic programs including *I Love Lucy*, *Leave It to Beaver*, *Gunsmoke*, and the *Tonight Show* hit the airwaves. Throughout the decade, TV went from novelty to ubiquity. In 1950 only 9 percent of U.S. homes had a television set. That number would ascend to a staggering 90 percent by 1960. With the NCAA and NBC in full partnership, college football also had its opportunity to gain a foothold with the viewing public. But with only one game telecast per week over the course of a season, it became impossible for all schools to receive exposure.

NBC broadcast a game of the week every year in the 1950s with the exception of 1954, when the NCAA package went to ABC, as the network outbid NBC by offering a 50 percent increase in fees. The contract was for two seasons, but the fledgling ABC Sports department did not have the infrastructure to land influential sponsors. They lost $1 million in just one season and were forced to pay the NCAA a $350,000 penalty. The contract was awarded back to NBC for the rest of the decade. In a near mirror image of the beginnings of college football from the previous century, when schools in the North dominated the scene, the South faced an uphill climb, and representation was limited. Throughout the decade, SEC schools were featured on NBC a total of 11 times. Notre Dame alone was on 12 times. Big Ten teams played on national TV 35 times. The Ivy League, even after gutting their college football programs in 1954, appeared 22 times on NBC in the 1950s. The SEC was at a decided disadvantage. Alabama, Georgia Tech, and Tennessee were the only conference schools to be showcased on TV multiple times. The other nine schools either appeared once or not at all.

ABC won the rights to broadcast the NCAA college football package for the 1960 season and beyond, but SEC schools continued to face obstacles in gaining the same exposure as programs from other parts of the country. The 1960 census revealed a doubling of the population in the seven states the Big Ten called home compared to the seven states that housed SEC campuses. But the conference was stuck with the NCAA plan they had helped create.

With college football on TV in short supply, the 1960s saw the proliferation of "coaches shows" popping up on local stations across the South every Sunday afternoon in the fall. When Bear Bryant took the job at Alabama, he negotiated ownership of game films to be included in his contract and created the *Bear Bryant Show*, which was picked up by affiliates all over Alabama. The new national ABC contract with the NCAA prevented schools from appearing on TV more than twice in a season, helping his show become, for a time, the highest-rated syndicated program in the country. Bryant insisted that his show be an hour long, giving him the opportunity to exhibit every important moment from the game that was played the day before. The show was so popular that the Birmingham NBC affiliate would often preempt the NFL game it was obligated to broadcast to put the *Bear Bryant Show* on the air.

* * *

National exposure on television for schools in the SEC was not the only area where the conference was at a deficit. By 1965, the most significant individual accomplishment in college football, the Heisman Trophy, had been given annually for nearly 30 years, and only two players from the SEC had brought the award back to the South. Frank Sinkwich, a halfback at Georgia, won the award in 1942, and Billy Cannon, a halfback at LSU, won it in 1959. Steve Spurrier would be the third to earn the honor, helping to usher in the next era of the SEC, and would remain a crucial character in its growth years later.

Spurrier was the son of a Presbyterian minister and grew up playing and loving sports, spending his teenage years in Johnson City, Tennessee. Basketball and baseball came more naturally to him as a young boy, but by the time he was in high school, football had become his favorite activity. As a self-proclaimed "late bloomer," Spurrier did not begin to attract the attention of college football recruiters until his senior year. In his final high school game, with his team in a 21–0 hole late in the first half, his head coach pulled him aside and told him, "Steve, you can throw every down!"[5] He ended up with four touchdown passes and nearly 300 yards through the air as he led a 28–21 comeback victory.

Word began to spread about the tall, lanky quarterback from the shadows of the Appalachian Mountains. He took official recruiting visits to campuses all over the South, including Alabama, Ole Miss, Kentucky, Clemson, Duke, and, naturally, his home-state school, Tennessee. With plenty of options and time running out to decide on where he would play in college, Spurrier refused to rush into a commitment. His father wanted him to play at Alabama for Bear Bryant. His mother wanted him to attend Georgia Tech because of its stellar academic reputation. High school friends and neighbors wanted him to stay in state and play for Tennessee. Spurrier himself was leaning toward Ole Miss because they had a successful program and he felt they had the best passing attack of any SEC school. But it was a message from a postmaster that altered SEC history forever.

The University of Florida entered the Spurrier sweepstakes late in the process when head coach Ray Graves got a note from his brother Edwin, a mailman living in Knoxville. After watching Spurrier lead his team to a win over Knoxville Central High School, Edwin sent a letter to his brother in Gainesville. "You ought to get this tall kid," it read.[6] Coach Graves traveled to Tennessee to watch Spurrier play in a high school basketball game and invited him down to Florida the following week to visit the campus. And from there, Spurrier was hooked.

"I enjoyed a wonderful visit to Gainesville. It was beautiful down there, with temperature in the seventies. And it was about 32 degrees back home."[7]

Tennessee made a late push to sign their homegrown star. At the year-end high school basketball banquet, Spurrier was offered a scholarship to play hoops at Tennessee by Vols head coach Ray Mears, but he turned it down on the spot, telling him, "Coach I really appreciate it, but I think my best sport is football."[8]

After ruling out attending Tennessee because they didn't throw the ball enough and Alabama because of a crowded lineup at quarterback, Spurrier selected Florida. He loved the weather, he had a built a strong relationship with coach Graves, and he said, "It was a school that had not accomplished much. I thought perhaps we could achieve some things that had never happened there before."[9]

For the first 30 years of SEC competition, the Gators football program was undistinguished, with zero conference championships to their credit. Even more troubling for Florida fans, they spent many of those years as an inconspicuous outpost on the southeastern edge of the conference boundaries. From 1935 to 1951, Florida had just one season with a winning record and had played in only two bowl games in school history. It wasn't until they hired Ray Graves in 1960 that their football fortunes began to turn. Graves had an impressive football pedigree, having played at Tennessee for Robert Neyland and coaching for nearly 10 years under Bobby Dodd at Georgia Tech. While at Tech, he was the defensive coordinator for the 1952 national champion Yellow Jacket squad and is credited with creating the modern use of the free and strong safety positions.

Graves had an immediate impact at Florida, leading the Gators to bowl victories in two of his first three seasons as head coach. By the time Spurrier arrived on campus, Graves had the program rolling, including a shocking upset at Alabama in 1963. It was the first-ever home loss for Bear Bryant as coach of the Crimson Tide.

With freshmen ineligible to play due to NCAA rules at the time, Spurrier saw his first action as a college quarterback in 1964 at the beginning of his sophomore year. Even though the Gators had an experienced senior quarterback in Tom Shannon, Graves began splitting the duties under center between his veteran and his crafty newcomer. Spurrier wasted no time establishing himself at the position, throwing for a touchdown pass on only his second career attempt. In the fifth game of the season, Graves named him the starter as again the Gators traveled to Tuscaloosa to face Alabama. Prior to the matchup the year before, Florida and Alabama had not played in 12 years. As members of the SEC, the schools had met only four times to that point. Graves approached Bryant before the 1963 season and asked to be on the Alabama schedule in order to increase exposure for the Gator program. Bryant agreed but only if both games were in Tuscaloosa.

In the 1964 battle, Spurrier and Florida kept it close against the third-ranked Tide, who were led by quarterback Joe Namath, but the Gators ultimately fell short in their upset bid, losing, 17–14. Even with the loss, Spurrier had proved himself to his team and coach. After the game, Graves said, "Spurrier's play as a sophomore under such pressure was incredible."[10]

The Gators finished the 1964 season with a 7–3 record and a second-place finish in the SEC. The following year, Spurrier had the quarterback duties all to himself and helped Florida to their first-ever appearance in a major bowl game as the Gators traveled to New Orleans to play in the Sugar Bowl against Missouri. Even though Florida lost, Spurrier threw for 353 yards, at the time a Sugar Bowl record, and for only the second time in his career, he played in front of an audience on national TV.

The 1966 Florida squad won their first six games of the season and climbed to a number seven ranking in the AP poll heading into a showdown at home against Auburn. The previous season helped bring Spurrier and the Gators out of obscurity, and the Florida sports information department was ready to capitalize on the hype. They put together one of the first national Heisman campaigns, keeping college football writers all over the country informed each week of Spurrier's exploits. With Heisman ballots due just a week after the Auburn game, Florida publicist Norm Carlson convinced the *New York Times* to send a writer to Gainesville for the game against the Tigers. It would prove to be a legacy-defining game for Spurrier.

The Gators would go the entire 1966 regular season without playing a single game on television. The only way the country—both fans of college football and the writers who covered the sport—was able to follow teams consistently was from the reports in local newspapers. Spurrier did not disappoint in his time to shine for the national media. Against Auburn, he threw for 259 yards and a touchdown, ran for a touchdown, and even punted five times. But it was a field goal that likely won him the Heisman. The game was tied, 27–27, with a little over two minutes left on the clock. The Gators were facing a fourth down on the Auburn 23-yard line and called timeout. Speaking with coach Graves on the sideline, Spurrier thought the Tigers would be expecting a fake field goal. He was the long-distance kicker for the Gators and had attempted two kicks earlier in the season. "Coach, let me have a shot at it," he pleaded with Graves. After thinking it over for a moment, Graves shouted, "Field goal!"[11] Spurrier nailed the kick. A few weeks later, he found himself in the office of the president of the university, where he was told that the 1966 Heisman Trophy was his.

Florida and Spurrier were thrilled to accept a bid to the Orange Bowl after the 1966 season, and they finally got their moment to shine on national TV. NBC broadcast the game, a win for the Gators over former SEC foe and eighth-ranked Georgia Tech in Bobby Dodd's last game as head coach. It was the first major bowl win in Florida school history. The 1966 season catapulted the Gators to a level of national prominence they had never before experienced. In the years that followed, Florida appeared on national TV nearly every season. But the NCAA was committed to maintaining their strict hold on managing the contracts with the networks on behalf of their member schools. Florida—and every other program in the country—was still limited to a maximum of two appearances per season. By the mid-1970s, the tense relationship between the all-powerful NCAA and some of its high-profile football schools was reaching its boiling point.

Auburn head coach Shug Jordan told reporters after the game that they lost to "Steve Superior," a nickname that would follow Spurrier the rest of his life. With all that he accomplished as a player at Florida, his role in helping the SEC become the dominant conference it is today was only just beginning. A new character in the drama, the "Head Ball Coach," another nickname he would soon earn, was still a couple of decades away from his debut on the SEC stage.

* * *

In the early 1970s, more than 600 schools were members of the NCAA. Many of those colleges and universities did not field a football team. Out of those that did, only about 60 were truly invested in performing at a high level. As Bobby Dodd learned a decade earlier when he unsuccessfully attempted to alter the common practice within the SEC of over-signing players during each recruiting class, the football powers were unyielding in their pursuit of victory. The Big Ten passed a rule in the 1960s limiting their schools to signing no more than 30 players each year. The other major conferences had no such regulation.

"If we weren't sure about a kid, but thought he might sign with someone else, we'd take him to make sure he didn't end up playing against us," Clem Gryska, Alabama's recruiting coordinator, said at the time.[12]

Powerful programs outside the SEC participated in the practice of "stockpiling" recruits as well. Legendary Nebraska coach Bob Devany explained his philosophy. "We felt there was a lot of sense in signing a large number of players. If you only sign a small number and you're wrong on a few prospects, you're in trouble. But the size afforded us a certain amount of safety."[13]

At the 1973 NCAA convention, the members voted to break into three divisions. Division I would consist of major football institutions. The other schools would have the choice to participate in either Division II or Division III. NCAA president Alan Chapman, a professor at Rice University, predicted at the time, "The association could have kept drifting apart because of the great difference between the large and small schools. No longer will the big guys be telling the little guys what to do or vice versa. I don't think you will hear any more stories about the super conferences."[14] It didn't take long for that statement to be proven wildly incorrect.

That 1973 convention changed college football forever. Even though the members were split into three divisions, they still retained equal voting power across the association. The smaller schools, feeling economic pressure to maintain their programs, forced the membership at-large to accept limitations on the number of scholarships that could be awarded. Gone were the days of signing as many players as a coach wanted. One hundred and five total scholarships, with no more than 30 handed out each year, was the new regulation. The football powers were enraged.

Shug Jordan didn't shy away from sharing how he felt when he heard the news, saying, "I don't know anything about hockey in Minnesota, lacrosse at Navy, Rugby at Cal-Tech, or fencing at Cornell, but I know that football at Auburn, football in the Southeastern Conference, has just been kicked in the pants."[15]

Others saw the new legislation as using economic factors as a cover for what the smaller schools were really after. "It was more of an attempt to level competition than it was to save money. It was being voted on by people who didn't have to employ such restrictions," said SEC commissioner Boyd McWhorter.[16]

The new scholarship regulations were set to go into effect before the 1975 season. SEC schools, along with many other football powers across the country, were becoming increasingly frustrated with their limited influence within the NCAA. But at the 1975 NCAA convention, Long Beach State president Dr. Stephen Horn floated a proposal aimed at television revenue that unknowingly galvanized those powers into an alliance. With aspirational goals of taking back some of the authority that had been ceded to the NCAA decades earlier, SEC school presidents began working with coaches and administrators across the country to see what could be done.

Horn proposed dividing the revenue generated from television among all three divisions of the NCAA. His plan would see that 50 percent of the revenue would be dispersed to Division I schools, while the remaining 50 percent would go to Division II and III schools. It became known by the big-time football schools as the "Robin Hood" plan, and even though it was rejected by the NCAA Division I Council, it convinced the football powers that something needed to be done before the smaller schools voted their way into the pocketbooks of the programs that earned all the money.

"The main problem was there were people who didn't have football that voted on football-related issues," Chuck Neinas, commissioner of the Big Eight at time, recalled. "To the NCAA's credit, it tried twice to restructure but it failed. Recognizing that, what happened was the group from the major conferences got together and said, 'Look, if we don't stay together as a lobbying group we will definitely be outvoted.'"[17]

Late in 1976, Boyd McWhorter, the SEC commissioner, met with leaders from other conferences and schools, including the Big Ten, the Big Eight, and Father Edmund Joyce, the athletic director at Notre Dame. The objective was simple: to establish an association where common objectives would be pursued by schools with similar ambitions as it pertained to big-time college football. With every major conference represented, the College Football Association (CFA) was formed and was ready to take on the NCAA.

But before the CFA would officially launch, its leverage would be decimated. At some point between the initial gathering and the first official meeting, set to take place in Atlanta in the spring of 1977, the Big Ten and Pac-10 got cold feet. Potentially concerned about going head-to-head with the NCAA, the two conferences that were joined at the intersection of the Rose Bowl in Pasadena bailed on the alliance. It was a devastating blow to the remaining members of the CFA.

"I always thought if we could get all the big schools together, we could run things. But I blame the Big Ten and Pac-10. They were the dogs in the manger," Father Joyce said. "[Both conference commissioners] were always in bed with the NCAA on all kinds of matters. And the NCAA was deathly afraid of the CFA."[18]

The CFA moved forward without the Big Ten and Pac-10. Initially organized to align on a variety of issues facing their members as it related to football, they quickly turned most of their attention to television. As a condition of the contract between the NCAA and ABC, small schools were guaranteed opportunities to appear on television in what was called the "super regional" plan. A game between major universities, such as Notre Dame and Alabama, would be broadcast to 98 percent of the country, while a game between schools from smaller conferences, such as the Ivy League and the Mid-American Conference, would be sent to 2 percent of the nation. Every team that appeared on ABC, regardless of broadcast distribution size, received an equal share. The big boys were growing tired of sharing the revenue.

From 1976 through the 1979 season, ratings for college football on ABC fell each year, dropping from an average of 10.04 million households to 8.7 million. It marked the first decline in ratings since the NCAA took over the management of the TV contract in the early 1950s. The members of the CFA were convinced that the drop in ratings was related to the smaller schools making appearances on national TV. And they were preparing to make the boldest move yet in the struggle with the NCAA.

Other than broadcasting the Rose Bowl along with a few other postseason games, NBC had been out of college football since losing the NCAA-controlled contract in 1965. In the spring of 1981, the NCAA signed a new TV contract for the 1982–1985 seasons, and rather than exclusively showing games on one network, they went with ABC and CBS, splitting the package for the first time ever. NBC was in the bidding for the package but was left out when the decision was made. However, the Peacock network was tired of sitting on the sidelines.

In August 1981, NBC and the CFA agreed to a four-year contract worth $180 million to televise college football, including a Saturday night game-of-the-week package. It was a stunning development and a direct affront by the membership of the CFA toward the NCAA. University of Georgia president Fred Davison, chairman of the CFA, announced that his members had until September 10 to declare if their games would be appearing on the NBC package.

The CFA contract guaranteed its members at least $1 million in TV appearances over the first two years of the deal. The agreement that the NCAA cut with ABC and CBS called for each school that made an appearance on national TV to earn $500,000 but with zero guarantees of an appearance.

The response from the NCAA was swift and decisive. Any CFA school that agreed to participate in the NBC contract would face a postseason ban from participating in all national championship tournaments run by the NCAA. Western Athletic Conference (WAC) commissioner Joseph Kearney summed up the feelings of those loyal to the NCAA, saying, "This was an exercise in greed and power. We may be deciding whether we are educational institutions or football factories. This has been a very sad day for college athletics."[19]

Rather than being a slight irritation, the CFA finally had the ear of the NCAA. "We got no real attention until the TV contract came up," Davison said. "And when we realized how little control we had over some matters, such as property rights, it made us all begin to think about how these things hurt us financially. We have to have more of a say, because [the NCAA] isn't going to come down here and bail us out if we fail."[20]

The CFA member institutions were given until September 10, 1981, to let the association know if they would be participating in the NBC contract. With only a month to make their decision, some were rattled, and others vowed to stay strong.

McWhorter tried to project an aura of calm in the SEC while simultaneously advocating for the CFA–NBC agreement. "I've heard no one in the CFA talking about breaking off from the NCAA. Rather, from the very beginning, we've tried to work within the framework of the NCAA. But this has been coming to a boil for a long time. Maybe we needed something like this to get people's attention; something like the story about using a 4 by 4 to get the attention of a mule. Nobody pays much attention to you when you are talking about not wanting the Hofstra's in the NCAA dictating to the Alabama's, but when you start throwing figures around like $180 million and $260 million, that wakes 'em up in a hurry."[21]

As the deadline approached for the CFA members to declare if they were in or out, the leadership within the association began to realize that the heavy hand of the NCAA carried too large of a threat. They were not going to have enough schools participate to make the contract work with NBC. It left only one final option to successfully break away from the NCAA to negotiate their own TV rights. On September 8, the University of Georgia and the University of Oklahoma filed suit against the NCAA.

Davison led the way. "Unfortunately, the N.C.A.A. has continued to threaten C.F.A. members individually and collectively with sanctions affecting not just football but all sports," he said. "In view of the N.C.A.A. position and the resulting confusion, it was determined that the question of ownership of a university's athletic program could best be decided in a court of law."[22]

After moving the deadline back multiple times for schools to declare their participation status, the CFA finally relented in December 1981. Only 28 of the 61 schools pledged their involvement in the TV contract, and NBC canceled the deal. If individual conferences and schools were to control college football on TV, it would be up to Georgia and Oklahoma to make it happen.

* * *

As the contention between the NCAA and its member schools became increasingly intense in the 1970s off the field, the battle for SEC supremacy every year on the gridiron was turning into a foregone conclusion. Stealthily switching to the wishbone offense at the beginning of the decade, Bear Bryant and Alabama turned their success in the 1960s into a sheer stranglehold of the SEC in the 1970s. The Tide won eight conference championships, including five in a row from 1971 to 1975. In addition, they claimed national titles from major polls in 1973, 1978, and 1979. They were awarded the national championship by lesser-known polls in 1975 and 1977. The 1970s was an unquestioned decade of dominance for Alabama football. It took a powerful running back from Augusta, Georgia, to not only end the Tide dynasty but also remind the country that the SEC was more than just Alabama and nine also-rans.

By the dawn of the 1980s, the University of Georgia had built a proud football tradition—but one where perhaps the size of the trophy case did not match the fervent passion of the fan base. Head coach Wally Butts and halfback Frank Sinkwich teamed up to lead the Bulldogs to Orange and Rose Bowl wins in the early 1940s. Sinkwich won the Heisman Trophy in 1942, the first SEC player to do so. The 1942 team was named national champion by a number of polls. Appearances in the Gator, Sugar, and Orange bowls later in the decade further established the passion for Georgia football. As Butts wound down his coaching career in the 1950s, the Bulldogs often found themselves in the middle of the SEC pack. More than 10 years went by without a bowl appearance, conference title, or national ranking in the final poll.

Vince Dooley took over the program in 1964 and quickly restored the luster in Athens, leading the Bulldogs to SEC titles in 1966 and 1968. The 1970s would often find Georgia as the bridesmaid to Alabama, finishing second in the conference five times. Incredibly, Georgia and Alabama, separated by only 248 miles, had met just four times between 1966 and 1983. The four games occurred as home-and-home series, with Alabama winning three. The matchup in 1976 represented the first time they would meet as ranked foes since 1946 and would not happen again until 2002.

Auburn came calling in the spring of 1980, hoping to lure Dooley back to the plains to take over the program at his alma mater. He turned down the job. "The overriding factor was I had too much invested [at Georgia]," he said. "I wouldn't leave. This has been my home for 17 years. I'm a Bulldog and proud to be one."[23]

Dooley was still searching for a generational talent that would help separate the Bulldogs from the SEC pack and propel them to that elusive breakthrough season. He would find it in Herschel Walker—and Walker would end up a Bulldog by the flip of a coin.

Walker hailed from Wrightsville, Georgia, and was the most sought-after player in the nation after rushing for an astonishing 6,137 yards at Johnson County High School. He initially had desires to join the military after high school. Having a difficult time choosing between college and the army, he decided to flip a coin. It landed on Georgia. Somewhat disappointed, he flipped the coin again, this time to decide between Georgia and Clemson. Again the Bulldogs came out on top. Thinking about the great tailback history at USC, he brought out the coin once more. "I flipped a coin between those two schools and Georgia won that as well," he said. "Then I pulled the names out of a bag and I pulled Georgia and then at that time I said I was going to Georgia. That's how I ended up at Georgia. Sometimes when you are naive and stupid, God will take care of you. Because that was the right decision."[24]

Walker rushed for 3,167 yards in his senior season of high school, scored 45 touchdowns, and was named the national player of the year by *Parade* magazine. When national signing day came and went with no decision from Walker, Dooley sent assistant Mike Cavan to live in Wrightsville until Walker signed.

The excitement of seeing Walker debut in a Bulldog uniform built up quickly among the Georgia faithful. Dooley did his best to temper expectations. "I really don't see Herschel giving us a whole lot of help this year. Realistically, I think he's going to have a slow adjustment period from Class A football. I think everybody, and that includes coaches, fans, and Herschel himself, will have to wait and be patient."[25] That plan lasted all of 30 minutes into the opening game of his freshman season.

The Bulldogs traveled to Knoxville to start the season at Tennessee, and playing in front of 95,288 fans, the largest crowd in SEC history at that time, they fell behind, 9–0, at halftime. Walker, who began the game as the third-string running back, was inserted into the starting lineup to begin the second half. Tennessee scored again in the third quarter, putting the Bulldogs in a 15–0 hole. But Walker announced himself to the SEC late in the third quarter when he took a handoff on the Vols' 16-yard line, cut back against the grain, and found himself one-on-one in the open field against Tennessee star defender Bill Bates. Walker ran right over him on the way to the end zone on a play that is still talked about in Athens to this day. He added another touchdown run in the fourth quarter, and Georgia hung on for a 16–15 victory.

The win propelled Walker and Georgia on a winning streak that would not be stopped. By November, the Bulldogs had risen to the second-ranked team in the nation when they met archrival Florida in Jacksonville. Trailing, 21–20, and facing a third down deep in their own territory with a little over a minute left in the game, Georgia pulled out a miracle to save their season. Quarterback Buck Blue, scrambling in his own end zone, threw across his body and hit receiver Lindsay Scott, who turned the short pass into a 93-yard touchdown. Larry Munson, the legendary radio play-by-play voice of Bulldog football, memorably and excitedly said on the air immediately following the touchdown, "Well I broke my chair. I came right through a chair. A metal steel chair, I broke it." The game had been selected by ABC for national television, the second time Georgia appeared in 1980 on the package. Due to the NCAA TV restrictions, it would also be the last time they would be shown until bowl season.

Georgia rolled through the rest of November with victories and rose to number one in the polls. A showdown in the Sugar Bowl against seventh-ranked Notre Dame was the only thing standing in their way to a national championship. With President Jimmy Carter, a Georgia native, in attendance, Walker ran all over the Irish, leading the Bulldogs to a 17–10 victory even though they completed only one pass. Walker suffered a dislocated shoulder early in the game but played on, rushing for 150 yards and two touchdowns.

Walker finished the season with 1,616 yards rushing, an NCAA record for a freshman, and ended up third in the Heisman voting. Georgia was named the AP national champion following the win, the first for an SEC team other than Alabama since LSU won it all in 1958. It marked the first-ever AP national championship for the University of Georgia.

Herschel Walker would lead the Bulldogs on an incredible run over his three-year career at the school, following up the dream season of 1980 with two more SEC titles. He finished second in the Heisman voting as a sophomore and won the award as a junior, becoming only the fourth SEC player to ever bring home the coveted trophy. By the time he departed Athens for professional football, he had amassed a staggering 5,259 yards rushing, setting the record for most yards in a three-year period. But with the NCAA still controlling the TV package, only eight of Georgia's regular season games with Walker in their backfield were broadcast to the country.

Thanks in part to his university president, Herschel Walker would be the last college football phenomenon to not have his exploits shown nearly every week on TV to the masses.

* * *

Led by attorney Andy Coats, a mayoral candidate in Oklahoma City who worked for the firm Crowe & Dunlevy, the University of Georgia and the University of Oklahoma brought their lawsuit against the NCAA to the courtroom in June 1982. Initially, both schools attempted to get other programs to join in and turn the case into a class-action lawsuit. But they didn't get any takers. Coats attended the NCAA convention leading up to the case and said, "We were like the illegitimate at a family reunion. Nobody really wanted to say hello to us. But [athletic directors] DeLoss Dodds at Texas, Bob Devaney at Nebraska told us, 'Gosh, we sure hope you win that lawsuit. But don't use our name.'"[26]

The argument that the plaintiffs brought before the judge was quite simple. They declared that the NCAA was artificially limiting the number of games shown on TV, thereby hampering the fair trade of the universities to cut their own deals with television networks, which ultimately harmed the consumer. Coats was shocked that the NCAA let it get even this far, convinced that they would settle before it went to court. Years later, Coats said that the NCAA stood for "Never Compromise Anything Anytime. We tried to settle every time we met. But they had never lost a case before."[27] Not only was the NCAA unwilling to settle, but they also continued signing contracts on behalf of the membership, cutting a two-year deal with cable newcomer TBS days before the trial.

The NCAA contended that they were doing what was best for their membership at large, namely, protecting the schools from losing money at the gate with the assumption that TV would hurt those figures and helping maintain competitive balance across the sport.

Judge Juan Burciaga of New Mexico had been assigned the case after the original judge, an Oklahoma graduate, recused himself. After two months of deliberation, Burciaga delivered his verdict. His 98-page report rebuked the NCAA on nearly every point and handed down a stunning defeat to the venerable association. "It reads like a damn CFA press release," NCAA president Walter Byers snapped when asked about the tone of the ruling.[28]

It was a devastating blow to the way of life for the NCAA. The ruling immediately voided the recently signed contracts with ABC, CBS, and TBS. The Tenth Circuit Court of Appeals stayed the decision, meaning that the TV contracts already in place would remain so for the upcoming 1982 season. Knowing that the NCAA could appeal, the CFA again reached out to discuss a settlement. Again, they were rebuffed. The appeals court upheld the ruling of Burciaga by a vote of 2–1. Again, Coats pursued a settlement with the NCAA. Even he understood that some aspects of the way the NCAA handled TV contracts was beneficial to all involved. "I didn't want to go down in history as the man who ruined college football," he said.[29] Rather than accept the olive branch, the NCAA pushed the case to the U.S. Supreme Court, where they were granted a stay through the 1983 season. *NCAA v. Board of Regents of the University of Oklahoma* would go all the way to the highest court in the land.

Arguments were made before the court on March 20, 1984. Three months later, on a blisteringly hot day in the nation's capital, the ruling was handed down, and college football would never be the same.

The Supreme Court decimated the NCAA, with a ruling of 7–2. "The NCAA's argument that its television plan is necessary to protect live attendance is not based on the desire to maintain college football as a distinct and attractive product, but rather on a fear that the product will not prove sufficiently attractive to draw live attendance when faced with competition from televised games," the ruling read in part. The NCAA's control of the TV contract "represented a classic cartel that restricted rather than enhanced the place of intercollegiate athletics in the nation's life."

After more than 30 years of strict NCAA oversight, schools and conferences were finally free to explore the open market and negotiate television contracts with networks. So what would happen next? "Even a lot of us who were involved," Dooley recalled, "were concerned about: Would this end up devaluing the game? Would it be too many games on TV? Would it have the effect of hurting ticket sales? Would it be overexposure?"[30]

Mere days after the ruling, the Big Ten and Pac-10 tried to put together a plan that would keep the football powers brokering deals with television networks as one package. But many of the CFA schools thought they could do better on their own, and the idea imploded. The CFA schools signed a contract with ABC, while the Big Ten and Pac-10 banded together for a deal with CBS.

Even though the SEC signed with TBS as a supplement to their deal within the CFA, revenues were down sharply. The number of games on TV had tripled, but the money coming in from networks had fallen drastically. Rather than having one or two games to pick from every Saturday, the options for viewers had multiplied. College football was everywhere, but the SEC and its member schools were suddenly in a budget crunch.

Faced with the prospect of having to create new revenue streams, the SEC began considering creative ways to stay competitive nationally and to prosper financially. Since forming in 1933, the conference had never added any new members. But the Supreme Court ruling put college football at the beginning of a new era, and the SEC was determined to explore all options to continue their quest for dominance on the field.

The First Super Conference

WHEN HARVEY SCHILLER WALKED INTO HIS FIRST NCAA NATIONAL convention in January 1987 as the commissioner of the SEC, he was immediately irritated with the seating arrangements. The representatives for the SEC sat in the back of the room, while those from the Big Ten and Pac-10 sat up front. After his colleagues explained that this was where each conference always sat every year, he devised a plan of action. A decorated colonel in the U.S. Air Force who flew more than 1,200 combat missions in Vietnam, Schiller was not one to passively let things stay the way they had always been. At 6:00 a.m. the following morning, at the direction of Schiller, a representative of the SEC showed up to reserve seats for the conference on the front row.

"You can't imagine how upset the Big Ten and Pac-10 guys were," Schiller recalled. "They said, 'We've been sitting at the front for years.' And I looked at them and said, 'Not anymore.'"[1]

Since the earliest days of its existence, the SEC had felt like they were taking a back seat to the other power brokers in college football. The Big Ten and Pac-10, conferences with schools in major metropolitan areas like Chicago and Los Angeles, had been exerting their will over the sport. As the years went by, the SEC had taken their own measures to build their brand against the wishes of the academically sanctimonious Big Ten. In the most visible example, the SEC did not restrict the number of conference teams that were allowed to compete in bowl games. In 1971, the SEC placed a record six teams in bowls. At that time, the Big

Ten was allowing only one school to play in a bowl game: the Rose Bowl. Every other Big Ten school was forced to stay home for the holidays.

In 1973, after playing each other to a 10–10 tie, Big Ten schools Ohio State and Michigan were unbeaten at season's end. The Big Ten took a vote from conference athletic directors to determine which school would play in the Rose Bowl. Ohio State won the vote, and fourth-ranked Michigan did not play in a bowl game. The Big Ten ended their outdated bowl policy in 1974. "Not competing in other [bowl] games represented a real recruiting advantage. The money was also significant, because the payouts were just starting to take off," said Wiles Hallock, the commissioner of the Pac-10 at the time.[2]

The verdict in the Supreme Court case in 1984 created a new world for university administrators and conference leaders. No longer beholden to the NCAA regarding television contracts, the schools and conferences were free to negotiate on the open market. But they quickly discovered that the market they were now entering was vastly different from than the one the NCAA controlled. And while the financial outlook had changed for the worse, it gave the SEC the opportunity it was looking for to seize control of their own destiny, build their brand the way they saw fit, and begin the process of moving from the back of the room to the front both financially and competitively.

The contracts the NCAA had signed with ABC and CBS, which were now void due to the Supreme Court ruling, would have generated $73.6 million for member schools in the 1984 season. With a splintered market, the networks pounced. The Big Ten and Pac-10 continued to work in solidarity and inked a deal with CBS for $10 million. The CFA also remained a unified body and signed on with ABC for $13 million. After partially igniting the process that led to this point, NBC stayed out of the fray altogether and did not submit a bid for either package. Televised college football games flooded the airwaves, but the treasure chest on college campuses that had been created by TV was dwindling quickly. "It didn't take the colleges long to realize that they had killed the golden goose," said former ABC Sports executive Donn Bernstein.[3]

Revenues for the SEC fell immediately. In the first year of the new open TV market, revenues fell from $11.2 million to $7.5 million for the conference. The impact was felt at all levels of power, as evidenced by Alabama dropping from $1.92 million in revenue to $764,000. With so many games on television, the price of a 30-second commercial plummeted from $57,000 down to as little as $15,000 in just a one-year span.

Still stinging from losing their court battle, the NCAA was quick to point out the negative consequences of the lawsuit. "It takes no economist to foresee with any accuracy what lies ahead. The networks are now in control of the market and they will seek to sell the most attractive product at the lowest acquisition costs," NCAA president John Toner said.[4]

But within the framework of the challenging new frontier, the SEC surveyed the landscape and began taking actions that would help separate their member schools from the sudden excess of college football on the airwaves.

The CFA contract with ABC called for games to be broadcast in the television windows of 4:00 p.m. and 8:00 p.m. Eastern Standard Time. The SEC recognized an opportunity to have games telecast in the noon time slot and moved quickly to sign an agreement with superstation TBS, which had become the most widely distributed cable channel in the country. After ABC and ESPN selected their games to broadcast each week, TBS was allowed to pick an SEC game from what was left over. With the CFA consisting of 105 schools, the contract with TBS meant substantial national exposure for the SEC.

TBS also offered a syndication package, and stations all across the South jumped at the opportunity to broadcast SEC football, even at the risk of alienating the national network they were affiliated with. WXFL in Tampa–St. Petersburg signed on with TBS and in the process preempted the Major League Baseball game of the week on NBC. "We are very upset," NBC spokesperson Steve Griffiths exclaimed when the network learned the news. Demonstrating that football trumps all else in the South, WXFL did not alter their plans to showcase the SEC.

"Regardless of what [ABC] and ESPN were doing, you could turn on the television in any city in the country and see SEC football, and that set us apart," Schiller said years later.[5]

With so much college football instantly inundating the public, even the networks were concerned about the possible consequences. ABC was especially upset after having a corner on the market for decades. "There's wall to wall college football from noon to midnight," Bernstein said. "From a network television perspective, that's too much. There are things that are not that healthy in the college football marketplace. But that's a fact of life we have to live with."[6]

On most Saturdays in the fall of 1984, only one Big Ten game would be broadcast, and at times, that game would be regionalized and shown to only part of the country. The contract with TBS meant that at least one SEC game would be seen from coast to coast every week, and most often, another SEC game would be on the airwaves of ABC or ESPN as well. While the revenues for each school were negatively impacted by the deregulation, the exposure skyrocketed. In the first two seasons after the Supreme Court ruling, Kentucky was on TV nine times. In the previous 35 years, the Wildcats had been shown on television only nine times. Auburn had five consecutive games broadcast in 1984 and seven overall, and the timing presented the ideal scenario for Tiger football to step out of the Crimson shadows, led by a gifted running back who answered to the nickname "Bo."

* * *

During the formative years of the SEC, Auburn football existed in an alternate universe in their home state of Alabama. While their bitter rivals to the northwest continued to build on their winning tradition of the 1920s, the Tigers floundered. The first 20 years of SEC competition brought very little pride home to the plains of Auburn: zero conference championships and only five seasons above .500, and, worst of all, they finished ahead of Alabama in the standings only three times. But the most pain was not found in the losing. It was that they did not have an opportunity to face their rival on the field. From 1908 through the 1947 season, Auburn and Alabama did not play.

Auburn won seven of the first nine games against Alabama from 1893 to 1904. When Alabama won the next two in the series, Auburn accused the Tide of using illegal formations. That led to both sides throwing around allegations of ineligible players being used, and they argued over money and referees. In the Alabama state legislature session in 1907, a proposal was brought forward to move Auburn to Birmingham. The proposal was defeated but did not halt future shots that Alabama would take at Auburn in the coming years. After a 6–6 tie in 1907, the series went on a hiatus.

As the years went by and the Alabama program found success in Rose Bowl victories and national championships, the desire to play Auburn became nonexistent. Alabama's Committee on Physical Education issued a report that read, in part, "We hazard nothing in saying that the game would not make a single constructive contribution to education in the state."[7] The time spent by administrators at Alabama as it related to Auburn was focused not on football but rather on trying to move the university closer to Tuscaloosa or fold it into their own campus system, essentially creating a branch of the University of Alabama in Auburn. By 1940, University of Alabama officials had grown frustrated with the amount of federal funding Auburn was receiving. Influential publisher and Alabama alum Harry Ayers proposed a plan to consolidate Auburn into Alabama "so that Auburn would become the dangling tail of a Tuscaloosa kite."[8] That plan was also defeated, and by 1947, state legislators threatened to withhold funding from both schools if they didn't play. In the spring of 1948, the presidents of both schools came together and agreed to resume the series that fall.

Part of the struggle that Auburn faced in the early years of the SEC was a lack of true home games. Because of a small stadium (capacity of 7,500) and a small town with limited public facilities such as restrooms, many conference opponents refused to travel to Auburn. So the Tigers were forced to play games all over the state of Alabama and even in neighboring Georgia. In the 1948 season, when Alabama finally was back on their schedule, the Tigers played "home" games in Montgomery, Birmingham, Columbus (Georgia), and Mobile. They played only one game that year in Auburn, stumbling to a winless record in the SEC, including a humbling 55–0 loss to the Crimson Tide in their first meeting in 40 years.

Fortunes finally began to change for the Tigers when athletic director Jeff Beard contacted former Auburn star Ralph "Shug" Jordan, at the time an assistant to Wally Butts at Georgia, prior to the 1951 season.

Jordan had carried the nickname "Shug" with him ever since he was a young boy growing up in Selma, Alabama, for his habit of constantly chewing on sugarcane. Jordan was a three-sport athlete at Auburn and became a decorated military hero for his service during World War II. Three years earlier, in 1948 Jordan had been passed over for his dream job when Auburn hired former Notre Dame all-American Earl Brown. "If they don't think an Auburn man can do the job, they ought to close the joint down," an exasperated Jordan said at the time.[9] Still stinging from not getting the job previously, Jordan had to be persuaded by Beard to apply for the job. He took out a piece of paper, wrote "I hereby apply for the head football coaching position at Auburn," signed it, and dropped it in the mail.

Jordan promptly breathed life into the Auburn program, leading the Tigers to the Gator Bowl and final season ranking of seventeenth in the AP poll following the 1953 season. More appearances in bowl games and the national polls followed, leading to a magical season in 1957. Starting the season unranked, Auburn rattled off win after win, and by the time they faced Alabama in the season finale, they were ranked number one in the AP poll. The Tigers crushed their bitter rivals, 40–0, clinching their first-ever SEC championship as well as earning the AP national title, only the second ever for the conference. It was an extraordinary and in many ways stunning achievement for Jordan and his Auburn program. The Tigers finished unbeaten and untied for the first time since 1913. They captured an AP national championship four years before Alabama would win their first such honor. On December 10, 1957, the AP general sports editor came to Auburn to present the trophy, and the festivities shut down the town. Declared "Auburn Day" in the state by the governor, businesses closed, and schools did not hold classes. A cold, blustery day on the plains didn't stop more than 12,000 people from gathering for the ceremony at the stadium. School president Ralph Draughon declared that the coaching staff "has done what I think is the most magnificent thing I know of."[10] Much to the delight and relief of Tiger fans across the state, Auburn football had finally shown they belonged in the same class as Alabama.

While that season would represent the only national and conference titles for Jordan over his 25-year career at Auburn, he nevertheless created an impressive tenure that enamored him to the Tiger faithful forever. By the time he retired after the 1975 season, he had accumulated 176 victories, and the stadium, which seated more than 61,000 at the time, was renamed in his honor.

When Jordan left the head coaching position, Auburn found itself in the middle of what would become a nine-game losing streak to Alabama. Following a brutal 0–6 finish in SEC play in 1980, the university turned to former Bear Bryant assistant Pat Dye to orchestrate the turnaround. The Tigers were searching for their first SEC championship since the 1957 squad, and Dye knew that the best way to accomplish the feat again was to find the next Herschel Walker. His name was Vincent "Bo" Jackson, and he went to high school in McCalla, Alabama. All Dye had to do was convince him to come to Auburn rather than play for the juggernaut in Tuscaloosa.

Earning the nickname Bo because he was like a wild boar when he was a child, Jackson was a two-sport star in high school and was drafted by the New York Yankees after graduating. But he wanted to play football and baseball in college, so he went about deciding where to attend. "I was an Alabama fan. I never knew where Auburn was," he said years later. The Tide had the decided advantage. But a huge misstep by an Alabama assistant coach altered Jackson's plans.

"My junior year of high school, a coach from Tuscaloosa came up to my house and said 'coach Bear Bryant sent me up here to talk to you and tell you we hope you come to Tuscaloosa to play. But I don't think you'll get to play until the beginning of your junior season.' I thought to myself, 'you gotta be out of your damn mind if you think I'm going to come there and sit on your bench for two years,'" Jackson said.[11] Pat Dye pounced on the opportunity.

A week later, Dye showed up at the Jackson residence. "I'm going to be flat-out honest with you," he said, "we don't have any running backs at Auburn. I will give you every opportunity to be a starter in my backfield your freshman season."[12] That was all Jackson needed to hear. He would play for Auburn, and his impact would be felt immediately. A record of 8–3 and a bowl win were minor accomplishments for Auburn during Jackson's freshman year of 1982. It was their win over Alabama for the first time since 1972 and his leap over the defenders on fourth and goal from the one-yard line that confirmed that the Tigers had finally returned to glory. Known as "Bo over the top," the play was a turning point for Auburn football.

Led by coach Dye and Bo Jackson, the following year saw the program reach new heights. Another victory over Alabama, where Jackson ran for 258 yards, wasn't even the pinnacle of the season. He finished with more than 1,200 yards rushing, and Auburn won their first SEC title in 25 years, capping it off with a Sugar Bowl win and number three national ranking. Auburn won the Liberty Bowl following the 1984 season and set up Jackson for a run at the ultimate individual prize in college football: the Heisman Trophy. By this point, he even had rival players gushing about him. "He runs with authority. He's aggressive. He can make guys miss him and he has the ability to go east-to-west and north-to-south. I'd have to say Bo Jackson is the best college running back I've ever seen," Alabama running back Bobby Humphrey said before the Iron Bowl in 1985.[13] Even though the Tigers as a team failed to live up to their preseason number two ranking, Jackson did not disappoint in his senior season. He ran for 1,786 yards (second only to Herschel Walker in SEC play for a single season) and won the Heisman in the closest race ever up to that point, beating out Iowa quarterback Chuck Long.

"If you're lucky, you get to coach one like Bo Jackson in a lifetime, and I was lucky," Pat Dye said.[14]

The foundation laid by Jackson proved to be the springboard Auburn needed to go on the greatest run in school history and establish the program as a national powerhouse. An outright SEC championship followed in 1987, with shared titles in 1988 and 1989. The Tigers played in nine consecutive bowl games from 1982 to 1990. Hosting home games all over the state had become a distant memory. Renovations to Jordan-Hare Stadium, including creating upper-deck seating in 1980 and again in 1987, had established a true home-field advantage for the Tigers as stadium capacity reached more than 85,000. Additional renovations were completed in 2004, bringing Jordan-Hare to its current capacity of 87,451. It is the tenth-largest on-campus stadium in the country. But perhaps the greatest success in the eyes of Auburn fans over this period was a dominance in the Iron Bowl. Four wins in a row in the late 1980s gave Auburn its best streak in nearly 100 years: they won six out of eight since Bo Jackson stepped foot on campus.

* * *

The SEC had now produced two of the most electrifying players college football had ever seen in Herschel Walker and Bo Jackson. The Supreme Court decision allowed more fans to watch Jackson play compared to Walker. Six games during Jackson's senior season were broadcast on national TV, double the amount of appearances Walker had over his final season. But additional exposure notwithstanding, schools in the SEC, along with other programs across the country, began to feel the budget crunch as the years went by, and payouts from the networks remained modest.

University of Georgia president Fred Davison had hoped that the ability to negotiate television contracts would help continue to fund athletic programs in general. "Title IX was beginning to put a pretty severe financial strain on our programs and football had to do it all, and football could only do so much unless we exploited it to a greater degree. I saw television as a way for us to alleviate some of the financial strain on our programs, especially in regard to the funding of women's sports," he said.[15]

Estimates showed that if the NCAA had maintained control of the TV contracts, an additional $200 million would have been distributed to member schools in the 10 years following the deregulation. "The drop in TV revenues had a tremendous impact on college sports across the board. It made the financial crisis even worse, and it didn't take long for everybody to wish we could turn the clock back to before 1984," NCAA executive director Dick Schultz said.[16]

By the late 1980s, the SEC knew they needed to act in order to give their schools the best opportunity to succeed on the field. "We're just trying to hold our own in what is a declining market," commissioner Schiller said in 1987.[17] But rather than turn back the clock, the SEC sprung into action to not only hold their own but also completely remake the landscape of college football forever.

Membership in the SEC had held steady at 10 schools for more than 20 years. Originally founded with 13 institutions, the conference did not seek to replace the three schools that departed previously, consistently turning down applicants that wished to join. Georgia Tech inquired about reinstatement to the SEC numerous times after leaving the conference in 1964, including prior to joining the ACC in 1978. "The ACC is the perfect conference for Georgia Tech. But historically we were a longtime SEC member and we felt like that had to be put to sleep before we could explore other areas," athletic director Doug Weaver said as they were set to join the ACC.[18] With so many changes occurring in other areas of college athletics, by 1989, the SEC decided the time was right to finally consider adding new institutions to their membership.

"The conference had been contacted by some former members, like Tulane," Schiller said. "And a couple of other schools contacted me and said, 'Have you thought about bringing us into the conference?' I started talking to the presidents about the chances of enlarging the conference for a variety of reasons, including territories, TV and so forth."[19]

Rumblings began to appear that the SEC was exploring expansion. April 1989 brought reports from newspapers across the South, even the *New York Times*, that the SEC was looking to add members to the conference. *The Gainesville Sun* reported on April 11 that the SEC was considering adding up to six new schools: three independents (Miami, Florida State, and South Carolina) and three from the SWC (Texas A&M, Arkansas, and Texas). When confronted about the reports, the SEC didn't back down. "Our school presidents have been and are discussing expansion," assistant commissioner Brad Davis said. "Nothing formal has been done, but it's a safe bet that it'll be on the agenda at the spring meeting. Everyone is saying, 'Let's see if it's feasible.'"[20]

LSU athletic director Joe Dean explained the motivation for considering expansion after standing pat for so many years. "TV has changed our world. You'd have to have your head in the sand if you don't think you ought to look at which direction you should go. The business of college athletics has changed so much in the last 10 to 15 years. [Expansion] needs to be studied."[21]

Even though Schiller was on record saying that "expansion is years away,"[22] by May 1989, he was also openly courting schools in the Sunshine State. "In the eastern half of the country, the key state is Florida, with its three great college programs, Florida, Miami, Florida State. Having all three of those would be a plus for the SEC," Schiller said. "Put this way: if Miami is interested, I would think we would want to talk to them. But we haven't invited anyone to our conference, and no one has asked to come."[23]

When asked about the potential for his school to join a conference for the first time in more than 40 years, Miami athletic director Sam Jankovich said, "If the SEC expressed an interest, we would go in with an open mind."[24]

Bobby Bowden, head coach at Florida State, was less enthused about the idea of his program joining the conference, calling SEC expansion a "cute little idea that someone comes up with every 15 years or so. They would never let that happen. They have a hard enough time getting champions as it is because they go around beating up on one another all the time. Why bring in schools like Miami and Florida State to make it harder? And why would we consider it? Last year we made $11 million on football and didn't have to share it with anyone."[25]

By the summer, Schiller was walking back some of his previous comments in the press and was now denying that the SEC had any interest in expansion. Perhaps trying to take the focus elsewhere, he began trumpeting a 16-team playoff to his conference commissioner colleagues as well as the administrators at the NCAA. His proposal failed to gain any momentum, and the SEC office and their member schools turned their attention to the upcoming football season without making any further announcements or decisions about expansion.

But while the SEC was publicly making noise about expansion, a much more discreet conversation was taking place in the Big Ten.

In the late 1980s, playing an independent schedule and not being tied down to a conference was a successful strategy for many football powers. Notre Dame was known throughout the course of college football history to be passionate about not belonging to a conference. Other schools had successfully captured national championships in the 1970s and 1980s following the same course. Heading into the 1989 season, Penn State, Miami, and Notre Dame accounted for five of the previous eight national titles. Miami won the national championship in 1989 as well, giving them three titles over a seven-year period. They had a record of 74–11 during this period, with five of those losses coming in one season. The Hurricanes were the unquestioned dominant program of the era.

As the television dilemma worked its way through the system 10 years earlier, Penn State had reached out to the Big Ten inquiring about joining the Big Ten. But with the conference firmly on the side of the NCAA and Penn State standing strong with the CFA, both parties knew the timing wasn't right, and discussions ended quickly. By 1989, the landscape had changed enough that Penn State again looked toward becoming the eleventh member of the Big Ten.

In the spring of 1989, Bryce Jordan, the president of Penn State, reached out to Stanley Ikenberry, the president of the University of Illinois and chairman of the Big Ten presidents. "I received a call from Bryce asking me if I would be willing to talk to a Penn State delegation that would fly up to see me," said Ikenberry.[26]

Penn State football coach Joe Paterno, athletic director Jim Tarman, and financial director Steve Garban met at Ikenberry's home in Champaign, Illinois. They traveled by private jet, and the meeting was held at night with only one staff member present, all to keep the discussions discreet. The Big Ten had granted the conference presidents the authority to act as the board of directors two years earlier, so Ikenberry saw no reason to include anyone outside that circle with knowledge of their discussions. He was the only Big Ten representative present. "[Penn State's] message to me was that they had a serious interest in affiliation with the Big Ten if there was a comparable serious interest on the part of the conference," said Ikenberry. "This was more than just a casual conversation. This was an indication that they had done some serious long-range planning."[27]

The contingent from State College pitched to Ikenberry the value that Penn State could bring in terms of television viewership. With a large fan base located in the Northeast, the conference could tap into a new region, which would increase ratings and create much-needed additional revenue for the members of the conference. All 10 presidents were on board and moved forward with creating a spot in the conference for an eleventh member. They had only one problem: they did all of this without telling anyone, including their own athletic directors or football coaches.

On December 14, 1989, only hours before going public with the announcement that Penn State would be joining the Big Ten, new conference commissioner Jim Delany delivered the news on a conference call to the athletic directors. The group was so startled that it was as if the line went dead. Legendary Michigan coach Bo Schembechler was pulled off the practice field for the call. He was also the school's athletic director at the time, and he was the first one to break the silence. "You gotta be shitting me."[28]

The internal pushback was so intense that the Big Ten quickly back-tracked and announced that Penn State was "invited in principle" to join the conference and that the final decision would be made at a later date after proper due diligence was performed.

"[The presidents] left that meeting in Chicago in the spring all in agreement that it should happen," Ikenberry said. "It was only after the news broke publicly that the divisions began to occur."[29]

"We had heard the occasional rumor about Penn State," said Schembechler. "We figured if it came to a decision, we'd be brought in to talk about logistics, scheduling and all the travel concerns and be given an opportunity to give our expertise. I was shocked because I never was even given a chance to think about the ramifications of Penn State being in the conference. It signaled to everybody: The party's over. This is a conference that is going to be run by the [school presidents] now."[30]

While Penn State officially joining the conference was on hold for the moment, it nevertheless represented the first invitation that a power conference had extended in the new era of college football. It also unleashed a game of panicked musical chairs among conferences and schools nationwide. ACC commissioner Gene Corrigan picked up the phone as soon as he heard the news and called Penn State athletic director Jim Tarman. "Why didn't you tell us you wanted in a conference? We'd have had you in a heartbeat!"[31]

* * *

Early in 1990, the SEC named Vanderbilt athletic director Roy Kramer as its new commissioner. After getting the expansion ball rolling a year earlier, Harvey Schiller left the SEC to become the executive director of the United States Olympic Committee. Kramer had been a top candidate for the commissioner post when Schiller had been named four years earlier, and now the job was finally his. After going on the record as against SEC expansion while acting as the athletic director at Vanderbilt, Kramer entered his new position as conference commissioner with a new state of affairs in the college football landscape.

Watching from afar as the Big Ten dealt with the internal fallout and public relations nightmare the presidents had created with their unilateral decision, Kramer and the SEC went about pursuing expansion with a completely different approach. In May 1990, the SEC let the world know that they were opening their doors to new members. The conference office announced publicly that its members had voted to pursue expansion.

After months of back and forth, Penn State was officially offered the invitation to join the Big Ten in June 1990. The conference office would announce that admitting Penn State was unanimous, but that was far from the truth. Ultimately, seven of the 10 schools voted yes, while three went against the plan (Indiana, Michigan, and Michigan State). Indiana president Tom Ehrlich voted no "because I felt that our teams traveling to Penn State was just too long a trip. To schlep to State College, well, it's not easy to get there."[32] (Penn State and the University of Indiana are 424 miles apart.) The Nittany Lions would be the only school the conference would add, and the SEC was determined to do more than increase their membership by a single institution.

Refusing to offer invitations before internal vetting had occurred, the SEC instead asked for programs that were interested in joining to contact the conference. "We had interest from Virginia Tech, Florida State, Miami, Tulane, of course, Texas A&M, Texas and Arkansas, and one or two others," Schiller said. "The presidents wanted schools that had a full commitment to men's and women's sports at the time. That sort of trimmed down a couple of the potential candidates."[33]

"We really wanted Texas," Schiller said years later. "So, something interesting happened: The [Texas] state legislature came back and said, 'If you take Texas, you have to take Texas A&M.' The funny part about it is that A&M was sort of lukewarm at the time about coming in."[34]

With the Texas schools unlikely to jump ship from their own conference, Arkansas, Florida State, Miami, and South Carolina all agreed publicly to be considered as new members. But it was Arkansas that presented the most compelling case, combined with an initial desire to join that the others lacked. Up to this point, the Razorbacks had a long and profitable relationship with the SWC. They helped charter the conference in 1914, but beginning in 1925, they were the only school not located in Texas. For the next 60-plus years, they were an outpost on the exterior of the Lone Star State.

While Texas had been the dominant program in the SWC, Arkansas wasn't far behind. They won 14 conference titles over the years and claimed the 1964 national title. Alabama was named the 1964 national champion by both the AP and the United Press International (UPI) polls with a 10–1 record. Arkansas went 11–0 and was named the national champion by seven different poll services, including the Football Writers Association of America. From 1958 through the 1976 season, Frank Broyles was the head football coach and the man most responsible for the success of the Arkansas program. He also had an illustrious tenure as the athletic director at the school and was the man in charge when the SEC began making waves about expansion.

In the spring of 1990, the SWC had concluded a controversial decade, with allegations of improper benefits being made available to players by boosters and coaches. Many were rumors, but some had been substantiated by the NCAA, resulting in teams in the conference being placed on probation. The most newsworthy example of this was the "death penalty" that was levied against SMU, forcing the suspension of the football program for two years in 1987. Mike Glazier worked for NCAA enforcement in the 1980s and said, "At that point in time, I think many would have considered football recruiting in the Southwest Conference to be, I don't know what the right term is, but almost [with] no limits."[35]

Broyles and Arkansas had also grown frustrated at the lack of fan interest at some of the bottom-rung schools in the conference. SWC policy forced schools to pay a guarantee to their conference foes when they hosted a game regardless of how many visiting fans were in attendance. Arkansas was often stuck with an obligation to pay $175,000 when fewer than 1,000 tickets were sold to fans from less successful schools.

"There was no magic formula to turn the tide back to Rice and SMU being the kingpins in attendance like they were in the old days," Broyles said of the schools in Houston and Dallas, which had become pro football towns. "There was no way to turn the clock back. How do you get the pride back in a conference with probations and a lack of attendance?"[36]

Arkansas felt that the less successful football schools were getting in the way of their advancement. Jackie Sherrill, the head coach at Texas A&M at the time, said, "I remember sitting in the meeting when Arkansas was going to the Orange Bowl to play Oklahoma and they asked for half a million dollars more in part of the pot [from the conference] for traveling expenses and other things. And you had TCU [Texas Christian University], SMU, Rice, who were not willing to give them the extra expense."[37]

Frustrated by their lack of status in the conference, Arkansas had become proactive a year earlier when the SEC first began discussing expansion. "Frank thought that Arkansas wasn't getting the considerations that they should get compared to Texas and some of the other [SWC] schools at that time," Schiller said. "So, he came to Birmingham, and we spent some time together with Doug [Dickey]," who was Tennessee's athletic director and Broyles's friend.[38]

Discussions between the SEC and Arkansas continued to occur as both sides weighed the pros and cons of an invitation being extended. With the excitement of joining a superior conference came reservations as well. Head football coach Jack Crowe said, "Frank [Broyles] asked me, 'Jack, what would you think about us going to the SEC?' I told him, 'Let me tell you something, Frank: We have a hard time beating Texas here. There's five Texases over there. Five.'"[39]

July 1990 brought panic in the SWC. Knowing that Arkansas had one foot out the door as they publicly flirted with a rival conference caused the SWC to attempt to circle the wagons during conference meetings in Dallas. Altering how gate receipts were split, eliminating the round-robin schedule format, and expansion were discussed among conference members. Broyles presented a positive outlook on staying in the SWC when he spoke with the media. "It's not just a possibility we'll stay. It's a strong possibility. The movement towards change was enthusiastic and encouraging."[40]

But even with the positive outlook stated publicly, Arkansas worked behind closed doors to leave the SWC. A meeting had been arranged for authorities from Arkansas, led by Broyles, and the SEC to meet in Memphis to discuss the possibility of an invitation being extended. As Kramer and his associate commissioner Mark Womack were set to board a plane for the meeting, the comments that Broyles made appeared in print and sounded alarms for the SEC contingent.

Kramer recalled years later, "When I arrived at the airport that morning, Mark asked me if I had seen *USA Today* yet. He handed it to me and there was an interview with Coach Broyles, and they asked him about the rumors floating around at that time. He very succinctly stated that Arkansas was a member of the Southwest Conference and had a long tradition in the conference and was presently an active member of the conference. I said to Mark, 'Do you think we should still go to Memphis? It doesn't look to me that Arkansas is interested.'"

Kramer and Womack decided to continue to pursue the possibility and get on the plane. They landed in Memphis, quickly picked up their rental car, and set out for a small motel south of the airport in northern Mississippi. The Holiday Inn, located in an unremarkable area, was the perfect setting for a clandestine meeting between the two parties. But Kramer was in for another surprise when he entered the motel.

"When we walked in, the lobby was completely full of television cameras. You could hardly get through the lobby. I said, 'Oh gee, somebody has let the story out of the bag, all the media is here to cover it,

Arkansas probably told their board of trustees.' Well, it turns out they were holding a northern Mississippi beauty contest. The cameras had nothing to do with us. In fact, they didn't even know who we were."

With beauty contestants in the background, the covert discussion went on as planned. Roy Kramer and Frank Broyles came to the understanding that the SEC wanted Arkansas to become the eleventh member of the conference, and Arkansas wanted to jump ship from the sinking SWC and align with the secure SEC. In the smoky back room of a small motel in northern Mississippi, the SEC had taken their first step toward changing the makeup of their conference and at the same time altering the future of college football.

On July 30, 1990, an announcement was made, and it became official: Arkansas would become the first team in the modern era of college football to jump from one major conference to another. Celebration ensued on the Arkansas campus, complete with Kramer wearing a hog hat and leading the assembled media and university crowd in a "Wooo Pig Sooie" cheer. The SWC was not amused. Conference commissioner Fred Jacoby said, "It's not good news. Arkansas has been a valued member of the conference, and we're sorry they are taking that position. They called me to tell me that their decision is that they are gone."[41]

Baylor head coach Grant Teaff was less diplomatic in his reaction. "I'm now thoroughly convinced that the Southeastern Conference is the Iraq of the college football scene in America," he said.[42]

The SEC now had 11 member institutions for the first time since the 1960s. And everyone knew they weren't going to add only one program as the Big Ten had done. Florida State and Miami were the top targets, with the Seminoles going as far as feeling compelled to deny reports in late July that they would be joining the SEC. But that didn't stop the rumors from flying. In August, Joe Dean, the athletic director at LSU, told reporters that he was 90 percent sure that Florida State would be the next member of the SEC. "I really think Florida State is coming. We've talked to their people and their president has visited us at LSU."[43]

Late summer brought more conferences to the expansion merry-go-round. The ACC announced that it would also begin considering new members and immediately set their sights on Florida State.

Bobby Bowden went on the record to give his preference, saying, "In regard to recruiting, we're definitely better off not in the same conference with Florida. From a football standpoint, we simply have more flexibility."[44] The Big East, a conference without football, announced that it would be looking to add both the sport and additional schools and locked in on Miami.

Florida State had been attempting to join the SEC since as early as 1955. Throughout the 1960s and 1970s, they enlisted the help of their rivals at Florida to gain admittance into the conference, and each time they were denied. Even with their past interest, by September, it became clear that Florida State would not be joining the SEC. Instead, Florida State chose to align with the ACC, wishing to create an easier path to success on the gridiron. Spurned by the Seminoles, the athletic directors in the SEC voted to not extend an invitation to Florida State. Still steaming from losing Arkansas, Jacoby made his feelings known again, saying, "The SEC was so aggressive, so overly aggressive, that it caused other conferences to defend themselves. They're acting like a jilted lover, a jilted suitor. [The vote] was a face-saving technique." Dean fired his own salvo as well, saying that "FSU was scared to play SEC schools," and proposed a ban on all conference members from facing them in the future.[45]

With Florida State off the table, the SEC was down to two final candidates: Miami, the most dominant football program of the 1980s, and South Carolina. The Hurricanes were the more appealing from a competition and demographic standpoint, but they were also a private institution. With the exception of Vanderbilt, the SEC consisted of large, state-run universities. Miami was also being courted by the Big East, a basketball-only conference that was looking to add football playing members to stay competitive in the changing college athletics landscape.

As September 1990 dragged on, the SEC became more and more concerned that they were going to lose Miami to the Big East. School president Edward Foote was quoted saying, "In the Big East, we have the highest concentration of alumni from that region, outside the state of Florida. To be able to play quality intercollegiate athletics in an area where we have lots of students and alumni is certainly an advantage."[46]

The Big East presented Miami with a financial package that allowed the Hurricanes to keep a majority of the TV and bowl money the school earned. It was too lucrative a deal to turn down, and ultimately, Miami chose to join the Big East Athletic director Sam Jankovich explained their decision. "We are an urban university, and we are not the South. We are New York."[47]

The SEC didn't wait to be spurned again by another school in Florida. South Carolina was a founding member of the ACC in 1953 but departed the conference in 1971 due to frustrations related to the recruiting regulations in the conference as well as a feeling that the ACC was dominated in administrative voice by the four North Carolina schools: Duke, Wake Forest, North Carolina State, and North Carolina. After nearly 20 years of playing an independent schedule in football, the most powerful conference in the South was ready to extend an invitation to the Gamecocks to join their conference. Days before Miami began to publicly lean toward the Big East, Kramer reached out to South Carolina president Arthur Smith. "If I call you back at 5 o'clock with an invitation, will you accept?" The two had begun having discreet discussions months earlier about the Gamecocks joining the SEC, and it was finally coming to fruition.

Smith responded to Kramer's question in the affirmative. "Should we make an announcement?" Kramer asked. "Well, I'll tell you this, as long as some of my board members know, we better do it right now or it's going to be out anyway," Smith said.[48] A press conference was called for later that day. South Carolina became the newest member of the SEC.

Now with 12 members institutions, more than any other major conference, the SEC was poised to take the next step in its quest to become the most dominant conference in the country. And they would exploit a little-known NCAA rule to move from the back of the room to the front. Forever.

CHAPTER 5

The Smartest Idea in the History of Sports

MAJOR COLLEGE FOOTBALL HAS ALWAYS MARCHED TO THE BEAT OF ITS own drum. While other sports, both college and professional, have long held postseason tournaments to determine their champion, college football has passionately and, at times, stubbornly stuck to the traditions of years gone by. Even as other sports, such as college basketball, began to see incredible momentum build and popularity increase for their postseason tournament, college football sat idly by, applauding themselves and defending their bowl games that followed the regular season.

By the 1970s, lower divisions of college football finally got into the act of determining a national champion on the field. Divisions II and III held their first tournaments in 1973. When Division 1 was split into two tiers in 1978, another playoff bracket was created, and Division 1-AA held a postseason tournament. But major college football refused to budge. The bowl system would have to do as a comparison against other properties, such as March Madness and the NFL playoffs culminating with the Super Bowl. It was a concept that college basketball coaches had a difficult time wrapping their heads around, and they let their football counterparts know it.

Legendary North Carolina basketball coach Dean Smith found himself on the golf course with a head football coach from the SEC and got right to the point. "Are you guys going to get a playoff in football?" he asked.

"I don't know," came the reply. "Everybody just sort of plays their season, then the bowls come in and pick the teams they want, and then after they play, they get a bunch of sportswriters together and they vote on who's the national champion." The football coach then asked a question of his own. "How would you boys in basketball like it if you did it like that?"

Smith, who would retire as the all-time winningest coach in college basketball, glared at the coach and shot back, "We wouldn't, because that's stupid."[1]

By the 1980s, a college basketball program could claim their season a great success by reaching the third round (the Sweet 16) in the NCAA Tournament without winning their own conference. In 1985, Villanova won the men's national championship by winning the tournament after finishing the regular season in fourth place out of nine programs in the Big East with a 9–7 conference record. An accomplishment of that nature was impossible to achieve in major college football. With more than 100 schools competing at the highest level and a limited number of premium bowl bids handed out each year, conference championships were both pursued with vigor and revered with pride. In the South, other than winning a national title, bringing home the SEC championship in football was seen as a greater triumph than any other accolade for the university athletic department.

"They tell me it takes a few years before you realize what you've accomplished. One day I'll come back here and look at Neyland Stadium and say, 'I remember the day we won the SEC,'" a jubilant Daryl Dickey said after quarterbacking Tennessee in 1985 to their first conference title in more than 15 years.[2]

In an ironic twist, the SEC historically played the fewest number of conference games among the power conferences. That policy, along with the practice of coaches being allowed to create their own schedules, led to conference champions over the years that had not faced some of the other top teams in the conference. As the 1980s came to a close, the SEC found itself managing increasingly difficult relationships between member schools and contracted bowl games. In 1988, the SEC officially recognized LSU and Auburn as co-champions. Both teams finished with a 6–1 conference record, but in the head-to-head matchup that year, LSU defeated Auburn. Since the conference named them both champions, the Sugar Bowl was free to select either team to represent the SEC in their game. Much to the irritation of the home-state LSU program, they picked Auburn, who were ranked 10 spots higher in the AP poll. The 1989 SEC season concluded with a three-way tie at the top, as Auburn, Alabama, and Tennessee all claimed a share of the title with identical 6–1 records.

The year 1989 would be the final time there was a tie at the top of the SEC. Roy Kramer had an idea.

Kramer was aware of a little-known stipulation in the NCAA rule-book that allowed for a conference with at least 12 members to split into divisions and hold a playoff game to determine the conference champion. When the SEC announced in 1990 they would be expanding by two schools, rumblings about a potential conference championship game appeared, but no one was quite sure what it would look like and if the SEC would actually add an additional hurdle to their own teams that were highly ranked. The conference was already in the midst of their longest national title drought since the NCAA began naming a consensus champion in 1950. It had been 12 lengthy years since Herschel Walker and Georgia won it all, and now it appeared that the streak might not have an end date.

Kramer had barely been on the job long enough to know how to get to his office when he marched into a meeting with the head coaches of the conference. His first few months running the SEC brought a flurry of changes, starting with the addition of Arkansas and South Carolina. With 12 schools, the SEC was now the largest conference in Division IA football, and Kramer was poised to take advantage in ways no one else dared to do.

In the meeting with the coaches, Kramer revealed that beginning in 1992, the conference would hold a championship game at the end of the regular season to determine which school would represent the SEC in the Sugar Bowl. After months of speculation, the new commissioner had officially placed one more barrier in the path to conquering what many thought was the toughest conference in college football. With the conference also deciding to play an additional conference game each year, moving to an eight-game schedule, the coaches left the meeting dejected and distressed.

"The bylaw was originally put in for Division III conferences, but it applied to everybody," Kramer said. "Once we hit 12 teams, we knew we could take advantage of it, and I knew it wouldn't be popular with everyone in the sport, even in our conference. But our teams having a chance to potentially play for two championships at the end of the season, the conference championship and the national championship, was something that gave a flair to our conference that was unique at the time."[3]

"The SEC will never win another national championship," Alabama head coach Gene Stallings declared as he left the proceedings.[4] As the new coach in Tuscaloosa, Stallings spoke with an added burden. He knew that national titles weren't just hoped for at Alabama—they were expected.

* * *

Alabama and Bear Bryant followed up their spectacular decade of the 1970s with yet another SEC championship in 1981 and an appearance in the Cotton Bowl. But the glorious run would end that year in Dallas. The 1982 season, with losses to both Tennessee and LSU for the first time since 1970, was a disappointment by Alabama standards. The Crimson Tide finished in sixth place in the SEC with a 7–4 regular season record and finished the season with an appearance in the Liberty Bowl.

Days before the matchup with Illinois in the bowl game, Bryant confirmed what had been speculated for weeks. The game would be his last one as head coach. "There comes a time in every profession when you need to hang it up, and that time has come for me as the head football coach at the University of Alabama. This is my school, my alma mater," he said. "I love it and I love my players. But in my opinion, they deserved better coaching than they have been getting from me this year."[5] Less than a month later, Bear Bryant passed away, dying of a heart attack at the age of 69. When asked years earlier where he would go if he ever quit coaching football, he quipped, "I imagine I'd go straight to the graveyard."[6]

With conference championships won at three different schools and six national titles, all at Alabama, Bryant left the sport as the all-time winningest coach, amassing a record of 323–85. He also left an indelible impression in Tuscaloosa, one that is impossible to overstate. It would take years for Alabama football to return not only to national prominence but to the top of the SEC as well.

"Whatever he had, whatever it was, he had a lot of it," said former Alabama quarterback Mal Moore. "He had something about him that people simply didn't have or don't have."[7]

When Bryant announced his departure, Alabama president Joab Thomas formed a special committee to search for their next head coach—a committee that did not include Bryant. The outgoing coach, who was hurt by not being allowed to have any involvement in the process, never made his preference public for who he thought his replacement should be. Ultimately, former Alabama receiver Ray Perkins was given the impossible task of following the legend. Perkins played for Bryant in the 1960s and was named SEC player of the year in 1966. He won a Super Bowl as a member of the Baltimore Colts and had spent much of his coaching career in the NFL. He left his post as head coach of the New York Giants to take over in Tuscaloosa and immediately faced adversity. After leading Alabama to a record of 8–4 and a win in the Sun Bowl in his first campaign, he presided over the first losing season for the Crimson Tide since 1957, the year before Bryant arrived on campus. A combined record of 19–5 over the next two seasons was not enough to satisfy the Alabama faithful who were starved for championships. With zero SEC titles under his belt and a 2–2 record against Auburn, Perkins went back to what he knew best and accepted a job as the head coach of the NFL's Tampa Bay Buccaneers following the 1986 season.

Much sooner than expected, Thomas again found himself in the unenviable position of looking for a head football coach to live up to the legend of Bear Bryant. Rather than hiring a coach within the Alabama family, he brought in Bill Curry, someone without any ties to the program. The move never had a chance to be successful, even though Curry played at Georgia Tech under Bobby Dodd and later was the head coach at his alma mater. His first two seasons in Tuscaloosa ended with Alabama claiming fourth-place finishes in the SEC, but in his third season, the program finally seemed to be back on track. The Tide won the conference championship for the first time since 1981, breaking the longest drought in program history, and Curry was named SEC coach of the year. But a top 10 ranking and a Sugar Bowl appearance were not enough to keep the pressure off the coach that so many viewed as an outsider. Losing all three games against Auburn didn't help matters.

"The pressure and the intensity of the scrutiny [at Alabama] is incomparable and indescribable," Curry said, reflecting on the situation years later. "There is nothing like it in college football, with the possible exception of Notre Dame; but at Notre Dame there's no requirement one must be a former player of Knute Rockne's."[8]

Immediately after the 1989 season, Curry was offered the head coaching job at Kentucky. In an unprecedented move, he took the position, going from the most dominant program in the SEC to a school that hadn't won a conference title since 1950 while under the leadership of Bear Bryant. Curry would lead Kentucky for seven seasons, never finishing with a record above .500. He was eventually fired, posting a record of 14–40 in SEC games. He never beat Auburn in 12 attempts as head coach at Georgia Tech, Alabama, and Kentucky.

Two coaches for the Crimson Tide in the post-Bryant era, two coaching departures of their own free will. Alabama, which had not won the national championship in more than 10 years, needed to get the next coach right. They would turn to a former player who Bryant had on his list to take over the reins when he stepped down from the helm years ago.

"He worked for Bear Bryant and played for Bear Bryant, and he is a lot like Bear Bryant. He expects nothing but the best from the people who he coaches."[9] That was what Dallas Cowboys head coach Tom Landry said about the new Alabama head football coach, his longtime assistant Gene Stallings. With big-name coaches, including Bobby Bowden and Howard Schnellenberger, in the running, the Tide decided to keep it within the family. Stallings played for Bryant at Texas A&M and coached under him at Alabama from 1958 through 1964, winning two national titles in the process. But having been recently fired from his position as head coach of the NFL's Phoenix Cardinals, Stallings had his work cut out for him to bring the Tide faithful on board. They wouldn't have to wait long.

The 1990 season, Stallings's first on the sidelines as head coach at Alabama, got off to a rocky start. They dropped their first three games, including losses to rivals Florida and Georgia. But things improved as the season went on, culminating in their first win over Auburn since 1985. They followed it up with an 11–1 season in 1991 and a number five ranking in the final poll, their highest finish since a national title in 1979. Stallings had Alabama on the cusp of returning the program to the greatness their fans expected. But beginning in 1992, an SEC team that wanted to bring home the national championship would need to win an additional contest, the SEC Championship Game, to make that dream come true.

* * *

As the dust settled on the SEC in the fall of 1990 and with expansion officially complete, the next steps for commissioner Roy Kramer included building consensus within the conference to get everyone on board with his vision and to begin to plan for a 12-team conference with divisions and a title game. It wouldn't be easy.

"If we are going to survive in the present atmosphere, we're going to have to learn how to change," Kramer exhorted the presidents of the SEC.[10] "We set out to make ourselves stronger and I'm convinced we did that." He immediately got to work on selecting a location for the championship game, hoping to debut the event at the conclusion of the 1992 regular season.

While the coaches in the SEC were approaching the changes with trepidation, the excitement from interested cities was the exact opposite. Even before the conference officially added South Carolina, the Peach Bowl in Atlanta let it be known that they would consider moving their game from the end of December in order to host the SEC Championship Game. The city of Atlanta was building a new state-of-the-art dome in preparation for hosting the 1996 Olympic Games and felt that they would have the perfect venue for the new event. By December, other cities, including Birmingham and Orlando, were rumored to be interested.

The conference was also evaluating the feasibility of playing the game at one of the three largest on-campus stadiums: Tennessee, Auburn, and Georgia.

Official bids were submitted in February of 1991, and the SEC received notice from five cities interested in hosting the inaugural game. Birmingham and Atlanta were seen as the front-runners, with Memphis, Orlando, and Tampa also seeking consideration.

A year earlier, the SEC was contemplating moving the conference offices from Birmingham to Atlanta. City officials in Birmingham reacted by committing to build a $3 million office complex at the specifications of the SEC and signing them to a 15-year lease, with the financial obligation being a microscopic sum of $1 per year. The response by government officials at the opportunity to bring the title game to Birmingham was equally swift. The city that billed itself the "Football Capital of the South" went all-in on landing the game. The Birmingham Football Foundation announced that they would shutter their 13-year-old postseason event, the All-American Bowl, to focus all their time and resources to securing the rights to the title game. "This is much more than a championship football game to us," said Alan Martin of the foundation. "It's hard for me to believe any other community could be as excited and determined to show the SEC how much we want the SEC Championship Game here."[11]

The other cities in the competition were busy expressing equal interest while extolling the strengths of their own locales. "We will certainly be major players. This would be an extraordinarily significant event for Tampa. We want it and we will be going after it," Tampa Sports Authority executive director Joe Zalupski declared.[12]

When Orlando submitted their official bid, they immediately grabbed the attention of not only the SEC officers but also the other cities in contention. Three hundred complimentary hotel rooms for the participating teams, use of the Florida Citrus Bowl stadium at no cost, free team meals and receptions, and a complimentary day at Disney World for players and official parties of the teams were all part of what Orlando was pitching to the SEC.

"I don't know what the other cities have presented, but I would think our offer would be hard for [the SEC] to walk away from," said Dylan Thomas, a spokesman for Florida Citrus Sports, which coordinated Orlando's bid. "The impact of Walt Disney World really gives us a luster that will be hard to beat."[13]

When Tampa saw the bid, they knew they were beat. "We can't give away the farm. That's definitely an impressive bid," said Rick Nafe, an official with the Tampa Sports Authority.[14]

After eliminating Memphis and Tampa, the decision dragged all the way into late May. Birmingham was offering $7 million to host the game, Atlanta was in the $5 million range, and Orlando had offered up Mickey Mouse. When the SEC presidents finally sat down to vote at their annual meetings in Destin, Florida, it was Birmingham that won the rights to the very first SEC Championship Game. It was not a unanimous decision, however. Votes from Georgia, Tennessee, and South Carolina went to Atlanta hosting the game. One lone vote from Florida was cast in favor of Orlando. But that left eight votes in the affirmative for Birmingham, which called it a "significant and historic announcement." Beginning in 1992, the SEC would crown its champion at Legion Field in the heart of Alabama.

* * *

Legion Field, known as the "Old Gray Lady" to many football fans in the South, did not have a permanent tenant in 1990. However, that didn't mean that the storied stadium was unaccustomed to hosting premier football games. When Alabama and Auburn agreed to resume their rivalry in 1948, Legion Field, with a capacity of 47,000, was designated as the neutral location that would host the game. Denny Stadium on the Alabama campus had a capacity of 31,000 at the time. Auburn Stadium, soon to be renamed Cliff Hare Stadium, held only 15,000 fans in 1948. Legion Field was the obvious choice. It would remain the host site of the game, which would become known as the Iron Bowl, for the next 40 years. Shug Jordan is credited with first calling the rivalry the Iron Bowl. Moments before playing Alabama in 1964, he was asked by reporters if he was disappointed that the Tigers would not be playing in a bowl that season. He replied, "We've got our bowl game. We have it every year. It's the Iron Bowl in Birmingham."[15]

Tuscaloosa sat a short distance away from Legion Field, with Alabama fans able to make the drive from campus in less than an hour. Auburn was on the other side of the state, and with a drive of more than two hours, Tiger fans never felt that the Old Gray Lady was a true neutral site. "Morris Savage, one our trustees who played on the 1957 national championship team, said it best," remembered David Housel, Auburn's former sports information director and later its athletics director. "He said, 'Legion Field was as neutral a location as Normandy was on D-Day in 1944.'"[16]

While both Alabama and Auburn used Legion Field for their own home games through the years, it was the Crimson Tide that played there most frequently, hosting at least three games per season in the venerable stadium. Auburn used Legion Field to host some of their biggest rivals, including Georgia Tech and Tennessee. The Volunteers did not play a game on the Auburn campus until 1974. But by 1980, Auburn had one of the largest venues in the country. No longer living a nomadic life, they were able to convince all their visitors to play at Jordan-Hare Stadium—except Alabama. When Pat Dye took over at Auburn in 1981, he made it his mission to get the Crimson Tide to play a game on the plains.

Having been a coach on the staff of Bear Bryant for nine years, Dye knew the situation all too well. When he bumped into his former boss within the first few weeks of taking over at Auburn, Bryant got right to the point. "Well, I guess you're going to want to take that game to Auburn," he said.

"We're going to take it to Auburn," the understudy said, confirming the instincts of his former coach. Bryant replied, "Well, we've got a contract through 1988."

Understanding that it could take a prolonged effort to undo years of tradition and that Alabama held the upper hand within the politics of the rivalry, Dye remained calm yet defiant. "Well, we'll play '89 in Auburn," he snapped back.[17]

Auburn announced in 1984 more additions to Jordan-Hare Stadium that, by completion for the 1987 season, would bring the capacity to more than 85,000 seats, making it the fourth-largest on-campus venue in the country. The Tigers had 61,000 season tickets sold for the 1984 season, which was more than the entire capacity of Alabama's Bryant-Denny Stadium at the time. With the close proximity to Tuscaloosa and the capacity of Legion Field being more than 75,000, the administrators at Alabama were in no mood to discuss moving the Iron Bowl out of Birmingham. But with the immovable force of Bear Bryant no longer on the sidelines at Alabama, the Auburn administrators began to make their move.

"We are just going to demand that Alabama play at Auburn when it's our home game," a member of the Auburn board of trustees told the press in December 1984. "There's no reason for it not to be that way."[18]

When told about the comment, Alabama athletic director and head football coach Ray Perkins shot back. "Demand? That's pretty strong, isn't it?" Perkins said. "I'm not going to worry about it. I've said in the past that the game traditionally has been played on neutral turf and that it should stay that way. They can demand anything they want, but that doesn't mean they are going to get it."[19]

Auburn stood their ground. "We're going to have a really nice [stadium]. In SEC games, we're supposed to be able to play our home games where we want to," associate athletic director Oval James said.

When Perkins left in 1987 to become coach of the Tampa Bay Buccaneers and Bill Curry was handed the reins, Alabama split head coach and athletic director into two positions. Former Tide quarterback Steve Sloan was given the opportunity to run the athletic department and was immediately thrust into the rivalry drama. In a surprising twist, Sloan took a restrained and more practical stance than his predecessors regarding where the Iron Bowl would be played. "When you look back historically when they started playing again in '48 the thinking was the game would be played initially in Birmingham and then would be played home and home based on the number of seats available," he said. "Whereas in the past Birmingham had far more seats, now you have a large stadium in Birmingham and a large stadium in Auburn and a large stadium in Tuscaloosa."[20]

This being the rivalry that it is, practical thinking rarely wins the day. With Auburn and Pat Dye sticking to the pledge of hosting the game once the current contract ended and bringing Alabama to the plains for the 1989 season, a new development occurred. In May 1987, Alabama produced a handwritten, unsigned notation from Bear Bryant himself. The school alleged that the note extended the series through the 1991 season. Auburn refused to give any credence to the revised document, with a source telling the press that the note was not signed and that "we are going to play the game in Auburn in 1989. If they show up, fine. If not, we'll consider it a forfeit."[21]

Amidst all the rhetoric, Pat Dye and Auburn refused to budge. They were committed to playing the 1989 Iron Bowl at Jordan-Hare Stadium. January 1988 brought a new twist. Using the handwritten note as evidence and frustrated that Auburn would not back down, the city of Birmingham sued both schools for breach of contract. With Alabama threatening to petition the SEC to have Auburn appear on their schedule every other year rather than annually, the Iron Bowl was in danger of not being played for the first time in 40 years. But after months of negotiation, a settlement was finally reached. In April 1988, a new contract between both schools and the city was agreed on. Auburn would host the game in 1989 at Jordan-Hare. They would play one more "home" game at Legion Field in 1991. After that season, Auburn was free to choose where they would host the Crimson Tide. Auburn celebrated, and the local papers hammered Alabama.

"The latest turn of events only fortifies the fact that the University of Alabama no longer calls the football shots in Alabama," columnist Bill Lumpkin opined in the *Birmingham Post-Herald*. "Coach Pat Dye and Auburn have ascended to the role once held by Paul 'Bear' Bryant and Alabama. Auburn is celebrating quietly and Alabama is wiping egg off its face."

Alabama would play their home games against Auburn at Legion Field for another 10 years before permanently moving them to Tuscaloosa. "When Alabama folks came down (to Auburn) and saw the atmosphere, and the tailgating and things going on in and around the stadium," Pat Dye said, "I knew that they would have to take the

Auburn-Alabama game to Tuscaloosa."[22] The Crimson Tide continued to host other home games at Legion Field even after moving the Iron Bowl to campus. But by 2003, with Bryant-Denny Stadium expanded to seat more than 83,000 and Legion Field falling into disrepair, Alabama moved all home games to Tuscaloosa. The Old Gray Lady would have to be content with the memories created in seasons gone by, and the very first SEC Championship Game was a memory that would echo forever.

* * *

The location for the championship game was set, but the game itself was still under fire. From both inside and outside the conference, opposition to the concept of having an additional contest to determine a conference champion was fierce. Some SEC coaches discussed contacting the NCAA to not allow the game to take place. SWC commissioner Fred Jacobs, never one to shy away from taking a shot at the SEC, questioned the legality of the game. "If this is just another way to add another ball game and make more money you have to ask what are the objectives of intercollegiate athletics. It could provide a significant recruiting and financial advantage for one conference."

Coaches from other conferences didn't know what to make of the new game. "There's got to be equality in college football," University of Miami coach Dennis Erickson said. "To play a 12th game, that was not the intent of the rule. That gives them an advantage financially and an extra game. It's almost like having an extra bowl game, which is an advantage to the league."[23]

Members of the postseason committee for the NCAA also expressed concern. "The danger signals are there," BYU athletic director Glen Tuckett said. "I do see some pitfalls. The bylaw was meant for Division II and now that the SEC game has come up I would think someone might want the legislation clarified or changed."[24]

Roy Kramer didn't flinch. "We see no problem with the game being played. There is always concern about new ideas, but this game will move forward."[25]

The bluster about the NCAA shutting down the game was just that. In the end, the coaches in and out of the conference and commissioners of rival conferences came to accept that the game was going to be played whether they liked it or not.

The additions of South Carolina and Arkansas caused additional consequences beyond the heartache of the championship game. The first matter of business that needed to be addressed was splitting the 12 schools into divisions for football. Ultimately, the conference was organized into an East Division (Florida, Georgia, Tennessee, South Carolina, Vanderbilt, and Kentucky) and a West Division (Alabama, Auburn, Ole Miss, Mississippi State, LSU, and Arkansas). Instantly, new rivalries were created and traditional matchups lost. With Auburn and Tennessee on separate sides of the line, a series that had taken place every year since 1956 would now occur infrequently at best. Florida had faced Tennessee only 13 times in the 57-year history of the SEC. Those two powers would now battle every season for the division title.

Another major sticking point to be addressed was the number of conference games to be played. The SEC had a long history of playing fewer conference games than their contemporaries, but now with 12 schools in the conference, they were forced to consider adding more games than they were comfortable with. In November 1990, the athletic directors voted for a seven-game schedule once the new schools joined the conference. Auburn, hoping to protect traditional rivalries with Georgia, Florida, and Alabama, was the lone program to vote for eight games. In December, the school presidents had enough votes to overrule their athletic directors and settled on an eight-game conference slate. The reaction within the conference was overwhelmingly negative, with the biggest complaint centering on the new edict hampering nonconference scheduling.

"An eight-game schedule makes it extremely difficult for the University of Florida to continue its longstanding rivalry with Florida State and renew its annual game with Miami," Florida president John Lombardi said. "We are disappointed by the vote but will work within the constraints of the SEC to resolve this problem."[26] Florida and Miami played every year from 1939 through the 1987 season. After a short hiatus, the two schools reached an agreement to resume the series in 1992. That contract was canceled by Florida before the game was played, and they would not face each other in a regular season game again until 2002.

Georgia head coach Ray Goff wondered about the impact the new schedule would have on the bigger picture. "I think it's going to be very difficult to win a national championship," he said. "Our schedule is such that we play eight SEC games, plus Georgia Tech and eventually Clemson. People say 'who do you play your 11th against.' Well, who cares? It doesn't matter after those ten."[27]

With eight SEC clashes to worry about within an 11-game schedule, Alabama openly grumbled about losing their ability to create traditional intersectional matchups. "Now we can't play the kind of schedule we should be playing. I think it's bad for us and bad for the conference," Crimson Tide athletic director Cecil Ingram said. "It doesn't make as much sense for us to play people like Penn State and Notre Dame now. That's a negative for our program, because we should be playing those kinds of teams."[28]

All the protesting both in private and to the media was done in vain. Roy Kramer had a vision for the SEC, and he sold it to the school presidents, who were now much more involved in the big decisions related to athletics. Longtime Tennessee coach Johnny Majors quipped, "Maybe the league presidents will get tired of us beating up on each other and go back to a seven or six game conference schedule. They could even go back to the good ol' days when we only played five conference games."[29] The clock would not be turned back to the "good ol' days." Kramer was thrusting the SEC onto a path of dominance that no one could have imagined.

* * *

With Roy Kramer and the conference office making so much noise off the field, the football programs were doing all they could on the gridiron to compete for national championships and bring notoriety to the SEC. Even though they had fallen short each year since Georgia won in 1980, the conference still provided many of the top teams in the country throughout the 1980s. But one school that had consistently failed to live up to expectations was Florida. The Gators would turn to a former star quarterback to help them finally reach the potential of which so many knew the program was capable.

After Steve Spurrier won the Heisman in 1966 and left Gainesville, he embarked on a 10-year professional football career, most of which was spent as a backup for the San Francisco 49ers. Spurrier played in 106 games as an NFL quarterback, starting 38. He threw 40 career touchdown passes and 60 interceptions. He also punted more than 200 times in his 10 years in the league. Following his retirement as a player, Spurrier somewhat unintentionally got into coaching, first as an assistant at his alma mater and then brief stints at Georgia Tech and Duke. With his offense setting records for the Blue Devils, he accepted the head coaching position with the Tampa Bay Bandits of the United States Football League in 1982. Again, as at previous stops, his offense mowed down opponents through the air. His success wasn't enough to keep the fledgling league afloat, and the entire operation shut down. Out of work, he began looking for his next opportunity. He was linked to jobs at Mississippi State and LSU but ultimately ended up back at Duke, this time as the head coach.

Spurrier proceeded to accomplish feats at Duke that were not only unprecedented but also thought to be impossible. In three short years, he took Duke from doormat to dominance. His quarterback, Ben Bennett, would leave school as the all-time NCAA leader in career passing yards and a school-record 55 touchdown passes. In 1989, he would lead Duke to their first conference championship since 1962 and their first bowl appearance in nearly 30 years.

While Spurrier was lighting the football world on fire with his Fun 'n' Gun passing attack in the ACC, the Florida program couldn't seem to get out of its own way. In the 20 years following his departure as a player, the Gators won only four bowl games, finished ranked in the AP top 20 only five times, and finished higher than third in the SEC only once. That includes the 1984 season, when they finished in first place but later vacated the title because of NCAA violations, and the 1985 season, when they finished tied for first but were ineligible to win the title because of NCAA violations. Many SEC coaches believed that Florida had everything necessary to become a dominant force in the conference if they could just find the right coach. In December 1989, they found their man. Steve Spurrier was coming home.

"We believe Steve Spurrier is just what we seek and desire at Florida," athletic director Bill Arnsparger said. "We all know what an outstanding coaching record he has. We feel he is the right person to lead this program."[30]

Spurrier was thrilled. "I'd pretty much given up on ever having the chance to return to my alma mater as Head Ball Coach because I didn't think the job would be open while I was coaching," he confessed years later. "So having that opportunity was a bit of a wonderful miracle."[31] He wasted little time with his opportunity, immediately getting the Florida program on track.

During Spurrier's first season, Florida was again dealing with NCAA probations from past transgressions, but the 1990 Gators gave the SEC a preview of what to expect for years to come. A 50–7 blowout against Oklahoma State opened his reign in Gainesville, and the Gators followed that up with a 24–13 win against Alabama for their first victory in Tuscaloosa since 1963. Even though Florida was not eligible to win the conference, Spurrier guided his squad to a 9–2 record and a final AP ranking of thirteenth. An early season loss at Tennessee and a defeat in the final regular season game against rival Florida State were the only blemishes. The 1990 Florida State–Florida game would be the first of an incredible 12 consecutive matchups between the two Sunshine State schools where both teams were ranked in the AP top 10 when the game occurred. The Gators and Spurrier had a record of 4–7–1 in those games.

The 1991 Florida Gators finally capitalized on all the promise and all the potential that had been building for years, arguably all the way back to when Spurrier was under center. In the final season of a 10-team SEC, the Fun 'n' Gun had taken the conference by storm. For the first time in school history, Florida had a perfect record during SEC play. They won 10 games for the first time ever and earned their first legitimate SEC championship. They even had a new nickname for their stadium. "I told Bill Arnsparger I think we ought to start calling it the Swamp," Spurrier said. "Let me talk to our marketing director," came the reply. When the response came, Arnsparger relayed it to Spurrier. "That'll never work. That's not a good name for our stadium." Spurrier was undeterred. "I loved the word swamp, so I just started calling it the Swamp."[32] The nickname stuck and is now prominently displayed inside the stadium, easily visible to all visitors. "Welcome to . . . The Swamp."

In two short years, the Head Ball Coach had changed everything at his alma mater. As the expanded SEC headed into divisional play in 1992 for the first time, the stage was set. The upstart Gators and Steve Spurrier headlined the East Division, while the West Division banner was carried by historic power Alabama. They would be on a collision course for the inaugural SEC Championship Game, to be played in Birmingham on the first Saturday in December.

* * *

As the 1992 season approached, opinions about the decision by the SEC to split into divisions and host a championship game continued to circulate. "Coaches Say SEC Graveyard of No. 1 Dream," a headline screamed coming out of media days. "I don't think there's any way any team from our league can be national champion," Ole Miss coach Billy Brewer proclaimed.[33] But while the gloom-and-doom predictions represented the feelings of the majority, not everyone agreed. LSU head coach Curley Hallman presented a positive spin on the new format. "If a team can go through the championship game and then the Sugar Bowl and get 'em both, then they might just win [the national title] overwhelmingly." But it was Jack Crowe, head coach of conference newcomer Arkansas, who seemed to have the crystal ball. "The SEC Championship Game is going to be the biggest football game in the country. And it's going to happen quick."[34]

Starting the season ranked ninth in the AP poll, Gene Stallings and Alabama began rolling off win after win. By the time of the "Third Saturday in October," the Tide had risen to number four in the country. Rival Tennessee kept it close but in the end lost, 17–10, marking their seventh consecutive defeat in the series. Road wins over LSU and Mississippi State in November pushed Alabama up to number two in the country. In the Iron Bowl, a swarming defense smothered Auburn, helping the Tide defeat their hated rival and send Pat Dye into retirement with a loss.

Alabama was now 11–0 on the year, but in the words of Stallings, they "hadn't won nothing yet." The SEC title game was standing in their way of a matchup with the top-ranked Miami Hurricanes in the Sugar Bowl.

Florida opened the season ranked fourth in the country but after two early season losses to Tennessee and Mississippi State quickly dropped in both the national rankings and the conference standings. But the Gators proceeded to rattle off seven straight wins and put themselves back in the hunt for the East Division title. A late season upset loss by Tennessee vaulted Florida into the SEC Championship Game, where the undefeated Crimson Tide awaited. Alabama was on a 21-game winning streak dating back to the beginning of the previous season. The last team to beat them? The Florida Gators, who handed them a brutal 35–0 beatdown in the Swamp in front of the largest crowd to ever watch a football game in the Sunshine State. It was Alabama's worst SEC shutout in more than 40 years. And now, to play for the national championship, the Tide would have to play in a game that didn't previously exist.

"They should have waited until next year before they came up with this game," Alabama cornerback Antonio Langham said before the game. "But they came up with it, and we're going to play it and move on."[35] He would be glad they did.

Even ABC didn't know what to make of the game, as they agreed to just a one-year contract to televise the nascent event. Renowned broadcaster Keith Jackson would be on play-by-play for the game, and he expressed reservations the day before kickoff, saying, "Conferences all over the country will be watching this one very carefully. But I'll tell you this, if Alabama loses it will set this concept back 10 years."[36]

After years of analysis, argument, and controversy, the inaugural SEC Championship Game finally got under way. With back-and-forth scoring and a shot at the first national title for the conference in more than a decade hanging in the balance, the game lived up to the hype. It was an instant classic. With the game tied at 21 and less than four minutes left on the clock, Florida, led by all-American quarterback Shane Matthews, was driving, looking to ruin everything for Alabama and the SEC. But Langham stepped in front of a Matthews pass and returned it for a touchdown, effectively clinching the victory for the Tide. The crisis was averted. Alabama would play for a national title in the Sugar Bowl.

Langham was Roy Kramer's new best friend. "There was a lot of angst even before the game, a lot of angst, and I'm not sure what the future of the conference championship game would have been had Alabama lost that first one and been knocked out of the national championship," Kramer said. "Our goal was for that game to serve as a showcase for the SEC, and I think we accomplished that."[37]

The first-ever SEC Championship Game was a huge success. With more than 83,000 fans in attendance, it also generated an enormous rating on TV. ABC was so captivated with the spectacle that they placed a call to Roy Kramer the following day asking to get locked in for a multiyear contract. Alabama went on to pulverize top-ranked Miami in the Sugar Bowl, winning the first national title for the conference since 1980. In the process, Alabama also sealed their first national championship since Bear Bryant brought the trophy back to Tuscaloosa in 1979. In the season that Alabama celebrated their 100th year of playing football, they fittingly returned to the summit of the sport.

Roy Kramer's vision that he turned into a reality would set the SEC apart from other conferences for decades to come. "The SEC Championship Game has proven to be one of the smartest ideas in the history of sports," CBS Sports vice president Len Deluca said.[38] Kramer was a man who a rival conference commissioner proclaimed "could always see the future," and for his part, he never questioned his creation. "I was 100 percent convinced the move to divisions and creation of the SEC Championship Game would be a success. I had no doubt about it."[39]

The SEC had succeeded on a much greater scale than many had expected in expanding to 12 teams, creating divisional play, and hosting a conference championship game. Outside the field of play, there was only one frontier left for the conference office to conquer in this new era of college football. Nearly 10 years earlier, the Supreme Court had opened the gates to television. Roy Kramer and the SEC were now poised to capitalize on the medium like no other conference in America.

CHAPTER 6

The SEC on CBS

THE YEARS FOLLOWING THE MONUMENTAL SUPREME COURT DECISION that gave individual conferences and schools the ability to negotiate television contracts was anything but the promised land that college administrators had hoped for. Their wish for autonomy had been granted. But the pot of gold at the end of the TV rainbow was nowhere to be found. In 1986, two years after the ruling, the CFA signed a four-year contract with CBS, while the Pac-10 and Big Ten continued to negotiate as one body and signed a similar deal with ABC. The payouts were 50 percent lower than the record amounts that schools received before they took the NCAA to court years earlier. Conferences began looking for an edge.

The CFA, consisting of the SEC, ACC, SWC, WAC, Big Eight, and independents such as Notre Dame and Penn State, was working overtime to arrange the most lucrative deals that provided as much television exposure as possible. But cracks were beginning to appear in the foundation of the organization that originally created the change.

With the newly signed contracts, ABC had college football coverage on the West Coast with the Pac-10 and in the Midwest with the Big Ten. They went looking for relevance nationwide and narrowed their focus on the passionate fans in the Southeast. Hoping to steal the SEC away from their CFA brethren, the newly appointed president of ABC, Dennis Swanson, discreetly traveled to Birmingham to meet with the conference. He offered a four-year, $24 million contract on the spot and left with the understanding that the SEC would accept. The deal would represent a considerable increase over what the conference was making in their CFA contract.

As word made its way through other conferences and schools within the CFA of the potential SEC defection, tempers flared. Threats of boycotting games against SEC schools and turning down invitations to the Sugar Bowl were made. Notre Dame stepped in to keep the CFA together. "I was furious when I heard about that deal," Irish athletic director Gene Corrigan said. "Everyone knew Notre Dame had turned down a big offer and that we could have gone out on our own at any point. Yet we thought it was better for everyone concerned if we stayed together."[1] In an effort to keep the SEC in the association, the CFA included more TV appearances for the conference, which would result in additional revenue. In the end, the SEC decided to turn down the attractive package offered by ABC and keep the CFA intact. But the ordeal was instructive for the conference and gave them an idea of what they were worth on the open market. With TV revenues continuing to stagger along, it was only a matter of time before a similar situation presented itself.

In the summer of 1989 the CFA again approached the negotiating table with the television networks. The contracts that had been signed three years earlier would expire after the 1990 season, and new deals were needed. Shifts in the sports television market were beginning to appear, as more networks were getting involved and advertisers were increasing their sports marketing budgets. *Sports Inc. Magazine* reported in 1988 advertisers had a 67 percent increase in year-over-year spending on sports marketing. Coca-Cola had a staggering 630 percent increase in their sports advertising budget. McDonald's was up 265 percent.

"The networks talked for so long about how bad things were and then they started paying huge rights fees," said University of Texas athletic director DeLoss Dodds, a member of the CFA TV committee. "What that says is the market place has changed. We expect our rights fees to double."[2] CBS came forward with a proposal to renew their contract at a rate of $150 million over five years. It was an underwhelming amount in the eyes of the SEC and other conferences in the association. CFA leadership was given permission to seek other offers. They were blown away with what they received.

ABC had already agreed to retain the rights to broadcast Big Ten and Pac-10 games through the 1995 season and made it known that they were ready to expand their coverage beyond those two conferences. ABC presented the CFA with an impressive five-year, $210 million offer. After nearly 10 years of searching for the promised revenue that TV would bring college football, the CFA had finally climbed back to amounts that had been earned before the court rulings. But the decision wouldn't be as easy as simply signing on the dotted line. Because ABC was retaining the rights to the Big Ten and the Pac-10, signing the CFA would create a regionalized broadcasting strategy. They would simply have too many games and not enough time slots to have national telecasts. Under the ABC proposal, most college football games would be seen only in limited parts of the country. The CFA would be forced to choose what they valued more: money or national broadcast exposure.

On January 18, 1990, the CFA announced their dancing partner. The money won out, and their games would be moving from CBS to ABC. David Ogrean, assistant executive director of the CFA, said, "This was clearly the best deal for a variety of reasons. But there's no getting around that in this marketplace, the bottom line is money."[3] CBS reluctantly backed away from broadcasting college football. "We were not prepared to triple the rights fee, which was the price requested by the CFA and apparently agreed to by ABC," CBS Sports president Neal Pilson admitted. NBC also submitted a bid for the CFA package, but it was even lower than what CBS put forward. For the next few years, the only place to see college football on network television would be on ABC—or so everyone thought.

Months before the final bids were to be presented and contracts signed, CFA president Chuck Neinas received a letter from Notre Dame executive vice president William Beauchamp ("Father Bill" as most everyone called him). It read, in part, "Until such a time as there is agreement from a network on the network contract, Notre Dame will not make an absolute commitment to participate. Chuck, we will simply not lock ourselves into a position that in the end might be harmful to our best interests without having all the facts before us. The University will only agree to such participation after they have seen the total package as negotiated."[4]

Neinas showed the letter to CFA colleagues, and it was interpreted as a mere formality that Notre Dame would fall in line with the TV packages once they were finalized. He did not share the letter with the networks. That decision would come back to haunt the CFA forever and would be the genesis of a new path for the SEC on television.

In 1988, Notre Dame won the national championship under coach Lou Holtz. It was their first title in more than 10 years, representing their longest drought since the 1950s. They followed that season up with a 12–1 campaign in 1989, winning the Orange Bowl in the process. Notre Dame football had never been healthier or more popular. Their matchups against Michigan, USC, and Miami were the three most watched games of the 1989 season.

Days after the ABC contract with the CFA was announced, Notre Dame athletic director Richard Rosenthal was in New York City for a basketball game. While in the Big Apple, he happened to stop by NBC headquarters and spoke with Ken Shazner, executive vice president of NBC Sports. Informally mentioning to Shazner some of his frustrations with the new CFA pact, including the plan to regionalize many of the broadcasts, Rosenthal left without anything substantial taking place. That all changed two days later.

After mulling things over, Shazner called Rosenthal and asked if Notre Dame would be willing to discuss breaking away from the CFA and signing their own deal. Rosenthal spoke with Father Bill and received permission to continue the conversation. Negotiations progressed very quickly from that point, and on February 10, 1990, Notre Dame shook the college football world to its core by announcing that they had agreed to a five-year, $38 million contract with NBC. It was a payout that would more than double what Notre Dame was set to receive as part of the CFA. Less than a month after helping to organize the CFA–ABC contract, Father Bill and Notre Dame bolted from the association they helped create. Suddenly, America's most watched network was partnering with college football's top brand, leaving anger and devastation in their wake.

At the news conference announcing the deal, Rosenthal defended Notre Dame's actions, saying, "We face a demand for television exposure of our games from fans and alumni all over the country. And after reviewing the details of the ABC contact, we felt it in the best interests of Notre Dame to seek a contract that would offer our fans more opportunities to see Notre Dame Football."[5]

ABC immediately issued a press release threatening legal action. "ABC intends to pursue all avenues to protect its agreement with the CFA from interference by third parties, including NBC Sports, and to ensure participation by all CFA member schools. The agreement was ratified unanimously by the CFA television committee."[6] Even though Father Bill had given approval as a member of the CFA, he never signed off on it on behalf of Notre Dame. "I sit as a member of the CFA. I don't represent Notre Dame. That's a very important distinction. We made it clear Notre Dame had made no commitment to the CFA," Father Bill said. "Each school has to sign on. We had not signed on. There was nothing other than the highest form of business ethics."[7] It was a tough pill to swallow for his CFA colleagues and contained more than a touch of irony for SEC schools, considering that a few short years earlier, it was Notre Dame that vehemently protested when the SEC was contemplating leaving the group.

"Father [Bill] Beauchamp never raised a concern about the ABC deal," said Glen Tuckett, athletic director at BYU and a member of the CFA TV committee. "He voted yes like all the rest of us. We all thought it was a good deal. We assumed his yes vote was a yes vote from Notre Dame."[8] Colorado State athletic director Oval Jaynes was less diplomatic. "The bottom line at Notre Dame is greed," he said. "They want all the exposure and all the money."[9]

Immediately following Notre Dame's announcement to sign with NBC, rival networks including CBS reached out to the SEC. The entire existence of the CFA was now in question, and the SEC called an emergency meeting to consider their options. "A lot of [television] people are talking to us," LSU athletic director Joe Dean said in a press conference after the meeting. "Our league is interested in seeing just what will shake out. An SEC television contract is a definite possibility at this point. We want to work with the CFA, however by the same token we don't want to get left at the post."[10]

By this point, Chuck Neinas was frantically trying to hold the CFA together. He flew to New York the day after Notre Dame bolted and promised ABC that he would get a commitment from every member within 72 hours. Suddenly finding themselves with the most leverage in the CFA, SEC commissioner Roy Kramer got in touch with Neinas early on in the process and told him that the SEC would need a guarantee of at least 20 percent of the TV exposure in the new contract with ABC. Neinas agreed, but the SEC had yet to formally bind themselves to the deal. With a deadline only hours away, Neinas got another call from Kramer. The SEC commissioner upped his ask, now demanding 24 percent of the exposures, and he needed it in writing. "Roy there is no way I can authorize that," Neinas told him. "But I'll tell you what I'll do. I'll unilaterally go to 22 percent and hope I can get the blessing of the television committee."[11] Kramer agreed to the terms, bringing the SEC back on board. The CFA signed a renegotiated contract with ABC and ESPN, although it was $50 million lower in total from the original agreement that contained Notre Dame as part of the package.

Roy Kramer and the SEC filed the ordeal away as a learning experience. "Notre Dame pulling away forced us all to look at the situation and decide what was in our best interests," Alabama athletic director Cecil Ingram said. "There were other folks offering us pretty good deals to go out on our own. We had to look out for ourselves."[12]

Twice the SEC had been tempted to bolt from the CFA, and twice they turned it down. Roy Kramer would not say no a third time.

* * *

The sports division at CBS has a proud history. In 1947, CBS was the first network to televise the World Series. In 1956, they began a "tradition unlike any other" by broadcasting the Masters golf tournament. CBS began telecasting college football as the first network partner of the NCAA in the 1950s. The 1952 Kentucky Derby was shown on CBS, the first time the historic race was on national TV. NASCAR began a 40-year run with CBS in 1960, and the TV home for the NBA was on

CBS during the explosion in popularity led by Magic Johnson and Larry Bird. Before it was known as March Madness, the NCAA basketball tournament found a home at CBS Sports in 1982. But the crown jewel of the sports department at CBS was the NFL.

Beginning in 1956 with a game between the Washington Redskins and Pittsburgh Steelers, CBS and the NFL worked hand in hand to bring the league into the forefront of the American sports landscape. The 1960s brought the merger between the NFL and the American Football League and the Super Bowl. In 1970, CBS was awarded the National Football Conference (NFC) games, which was home to the majority of the larger TV markets in the league and was seen as the premium package. By the 1980s, the NFL had exploded in popularity and surpassed Major League Baseball as the most watched sport in the country.

With such a heavy emphasis on showcasing NFL games every Sunday, CBS didn't pursue contracts with college football entities such as the CFA with much concern. Throughout the 1960s and 1970s, CBS put bowl games like the Sun Bowl and the Fiesta Bowl on their airwaves and had a short stint as a partner with the NCAA in 1982 and 1983. After the Supreme Court deregulated college football on TV, CBS signed deals with the Big Ten and the Pac-10 in 1984 and then swapped with ABC in 1987, picking up the CFA contract. But when it came to football, the priority at CBS Sports throughout this period was always on the NFL. In December 1993, an Australian maverick named Rupert Murdoch altered the level of priority CBS placed on college football.

Murdoch and his company, News Corporation, owned the upstart Fox Television Network. Fox was launched in 1986 but struggled in their early years to gain credibility as a true competitor to the "Big Three" (CBS, NBC, and ABC). Murdoch saw the NFL as his ticket into the mainstream of American media. The NFC contract with CBS was coming to an end at the conclusion of the 1993 season, and Murdoch made his move. Mired in a ratings downturn, CBS wasn't prepared to offer a large increase to the NFL for a new contract, and Murdoch pounced. With CBS taking for granted that the NFL would never leave for another network, Fox swooped in and made an offer that blew away everyone involved in sports television, proposing a deal for $1.6 billion over four years. Representing a $500 million increase from the previous contract that CBS had for the NFC, it was an astronomical amount for a network to promise for sports programming.

Many industry insiders commended the restraint of CBS and questioned the judgment of Fox at the time. Mick Schafbuch, former chairman of the CBS affiliate board, said, "I know that's what Fox believed it had to do to take the network to the next level of credibility, but you have to ask yourself, was that really the best way to spend their money? What would $1.6 billion spent on primetime programming and promotion have gotten them instead?"[3]

CBS had been bickering internally, questioning if they should raise their offer to just shy of $300 million per year when they received the news about the Fox bid. "Peter Lund [CBS executive vice president] came back up to the room and he was white as a sheet," said CBS Sports president Neil Pilson. "He said, 'You got to sit down, everybody. You're not going to believe this. But the league has a $400 million-a-year offer from Fox for our package.'" It was such a huge amount to commit that even the NFL was questioning it. Dallas Cowboys owner Jerry Jones said, "It was aggressive enough that one of the biggest questions was, 'Can they pay this?' As a matter of fact, there were several owners who said, 'We need to get some lines of credit here to back this up.'"[14] In the end, the NFL had no choice but to accept the offer from Fox. For the first time since 1955, CBS would not have broadcast rights to professional football.

Having also recently lost their rights to Major League Baseball in addition to the NFL, CBS Sports was on the hunt for new sports properties to bring to the network to fill airtime. With money to spend and the latest CFA contract nearing completion, CBS reached out to Roy Kramer and the SEC to gauge the interest of the league in leaving the association and cutting their own deal with CBS. At $85 million and with a five-year contract, Kramer had no choice but to listen.

In a replication of the events that took place with Notre Dame and the previous contract with ABC and ESPN, the CFA was at a crossroads, only this time it was the SEC in the line of fire. Roy Kramer was the chair of the CFA television committee in the winter of 1994, and much like Father Bill a few years earlier, he was bombarded with threats when news broke of the offer from CBS.

Future schedules, the SEC Championship Game, and revenue from the NCAA basketball contract all became targets. "You can throw schedules out the window," a rival conference official told the *Atlanta Journal-Constitution* at the time, "because nobody wants to play [the SEC]. [The other leagues] are going to freeze them out. [The SEC Championship Game] could easily be voted out on the NCAA convention floor," the official said. "The playoff creates a competitive disadvantage. You have no idea the money left on the table if the SEC goes to CBS."[15]

For the SEC, signing the deal with CBS represented more than simply an opportunity to pad athletic department bank accounts within the conference. Having grown tired of sharing the spotlight with the Big Ten, the SEC was looking for additional exposure as well. "There's a certain amount of disgruntlement that the SEC has had to share airtime with the Big Ten that the games they think are of national importance are being shown regionally," said a cable television executive. "Coaches have complained that the Big Ten has a recruiting advantage because of the way they're exposed on ABC."[16]

Roy Kramer ignored the noise from outside influences, and on February 12, 1994, the deal became official. Along with the Big East Conference, the SEC would be leaving the CFA, with broadcasts beginning in the 1996 season, to sign a contract with CBS. The payout would more than double what the SEC would have received from the contract that ABC was offering the CFA and would immediately increase the SEC's annual payout to its schools from $45.5 million to $58.9 million. "I know there were hard feelings, but my primary loyalty was to the Southeastern Conference," Roy Kramer said. "[The contract with CBS] gave us a market place to be exposed on a national television network that no other conference had at the time."[17]

The SEC contract with CBS effectively put the CFA out of business. The Big 12 and the ACC agreed to their own separate contracts with ABC, but in doing so, they were forced to share airtime with the Big Ten and the Pac-10, limiting their appearances nationally. ABC stood by their strategy of regionalizing college football broadcasts and openly questioned what CBS was attempting with the SEC. "It's clearly good for CBS in a restricted portion of the country, say the 20 percent of the country that the SEC encompasses," said David Downs, vice president for programming at ABC. "It might be hard to get an affiliate in Colorado salivating about the LSU-Tennessee game."[18]

Rival leagues continued to shower Roy Kramer with complaints. "There is a point where there just may be too much [college football on television] and I think we may have reached that point with these packages," grumbled ACC commissioner Gene Corrigan, who was one of the most vocal opponents of the SEC signing a contract with CBS.

Never one to panic, the seasoned SEC commissioner stood his ground. "It is difficult for me to understand how anybody could be hurt by this," Kramer said. "Everybody is receiving more money from television than they were before. Everybody is getting much more exposure. A lot of schools that were not getting exposed on national television are now getting exposed."[19]

As the 1996 college football season approached, CBS Sports began making preparations for their first season broadcasting the SEC. From hiring announcers to determining which games they would select to cover, assembling the production had begun. Fortunately, the theme music was one item that they already had in their possession. Leading up to telecasting the 1987 Super Bowl, CBS went looking for introduction music to kick off their broadcast of the NFL's premier event. CBS Sports executive Doug Towey asked production company contacts to send him arrangements to choose from. He came across a song written by New York City resident and Giants fan Lloyd Landesman. Towey selected the song, which was composed in only eight hours and was never given a name. Little did Landesman know that the song that was inspired by the Army–Navy games he attended when he was a kid would endure for decades—only not in the NFL.

"I was excited it was going to be on and anxiously awaiting the game," Landesman recalled. "Of course, the Giants were in that Super Bowl, so it was kind of a double positive experience. But I thought it was a one-time play."[20]

Following the Super Bowl, CBS Sports began using the song for every college football broadcast on the network beginning with the 1987 season. When they picked up the rights to the SEC in 1996, it was only natural that they continued using it as an introduction on telecasts for their new college football partner. Even though CBS Sports has continued to use the song over the years on all college football broadcasts, including those of bowl games and other conferences, the music that Landesman wrote became synonymous with the SEC.

"The way it's composed, it sounds like college football," CBS Sports chairman Sean McManus said years later. "It probably wouldn't be appropriate for NFL football or other pro sports, but it really sounds like a Saturday afternoon. For some reason it just resonates with your mind, and either consciously or subconsciously, you remember some of the great games this music has surrounded."[21]

With the theme music in place, CBS went to work on the announcing team that would cover the games. And just like the theme song, the play-by-play announcer who eventually settled into the role was an NFL broadcaster already with the network. There was just one problem: Verne Lundquist wanted nothing to do with college football at this point in his career.

On September 7, 1996, the versatile Jim Nantz welcomed viewers to the very first CBS Sports broadcast under their new contract with the SEC. The game was held in a sold-out stadium in Knoxville, where the UCLA Bruins would be facing the Tennessee Volunteers in front of more than 100,000 people. Nantz was paired with analyst Terry Donahue, the recently retired college coach. By the 1997 season, the talented Sean McDonough took over play-by-play duties and was eventually teamed with former Penn State and NFL quarterback Todd Blackledge. Lundquist, who had covered college football in the past, was at this time the number two announcer for CBS on their NFL coverage. A conversation with CBS Sports president Sean McManus changed everything for Lundquist.

Legendary announcer Dick Enberg was contemplating a move from NBC, where he had been for years, over to CBS when McManus posed a question to Lundquist that would change his career.

"In the unlikely event Enberg comes over [to CBS]," McManus asked, "how would you feel about switching back to college football and becoming the lead voice on the SEC?" In his autobiography, Lundquist confessed that he didn't feel great about it. "I said all the right things [to McManus], however in the back of my mind, I saw this as a demotion. I hung up the phone, turned to my wife, and said, 'Honey, pack your bags for Tuscaloosa.'"22

The intuition that Lundquist had during his conversation with McManus proved correct. Enberg joined CBS, and beginning with the 2000 season, Lundquist became the lead announcer for the SEC on CBS. But rather than the move negatively impacting his career, Lundquist would be the voice that millions would hear in their living room as they watched the SEC rise to heights never before seen by any conference.

"Making the move to the SEC was the most significant assignment in my career," Lundquist recalled years later. "CBS exposed the rest of the country to what had been going on below the Mason-Dixon Line for all those years. More than anything else I've done, I believe folks will remember me for having covered the SEC."23

It was impossible at the time to predict the advantages the SEC would gain over other conferences due to their new partnership with CBS. They would be the only conference to have an exclusive presence every week with a national broadcast on network television. South Carolina athletic director Mike McGee proved prescient when he said, "It's not 'College Football on CBS,' it's 'The SEC on CBS.' You have a national stage that, in many respects, far outstrips the rest of the conferences."24 The SEC was poised to fill that stage with college football's best teams and dominate the sport in the years ahead.

* * *

Between 1981, the season following Georgia's national championship, and the 1995 season, the only time an SEC team finished number one in the country was Alabama in 1992. But by the mid-1990s, the SEC had made wholesale changes in the way football was governed within the conference. They led the way in expansion when they added South Carolina and Arkansas. They became the first conference to hold a championship game, which, despite the naysayers, had turned into an enormous success both financially and competitively. And now the SEC had an exclusive broadcasting home on network television due to their partnership with CBS. The long droughts between national championships would quickly evaporate, beginning where only Gators get out alive.

Florida and Steve Spurrier participated in the inaugural SEC Championship Game in 1992, losing to Alabama, the eventual national champions. But the Head Ball Coach was just getting started building a powerhouse in Gainesville. The 1993 season ended with the same two teams in Birmingham playing for the conference title, but this time, the Gators went home with the trophy, as they had little trouble with Alabama in a 28–13 victory. After zero conference championships in school history, Florida now had two in a three-year period. A 41–7 thrashing of West Virginia in the Sugar Bowl gave the Gators a final ranking in the top five of the AP poll for the first time in school history in a non-probation season.

After playing the first two SEC Championship Games in Birmingham, the 1994 version would be heading to a new home, the Georgia Dome in Atlanta. Although the SEC had originally signed a five-year deal for the game to be played at Legion Field, a clause allowed the conference to move the game at any point if the city of Birmingham did not meet the promised financial obligations. Following the 1993 title game, the city came up $300,000 short in its payment to the conference. Concerns about weather (the first two games were played in freezing temperatures and rain) and Legion Field not being a true neutral site also were factors. The league voted, 8–4, to move the game, with Alabama, Auburn, LSU, and Kentucky opposing. Birmingham was devastated by the decision.

"I am shocked that the city was not given an opportunity to discuss the decision further with the commissioner before it was made final," Birmingham mayor Richard Arrington said. "Given the efforts put forth to accommodate the league's every request to enhance Birmingham as a site for the SEC championship game, I cannot help but feel that we have not been dealt with fairly in this matter."[25]

The move to Atlanta would turn out to be an enormous success, with the SEC Championship Game staying at the Georgia Dome through the 2016 season. Beginning in 2017, the title game was hosted by Mercedes-Benz Stadium, a state-of-the-art venue built by the city of Atlanta to replace the Georgia Dome. Going back to 1994, every SEC team begins their season aiming for a date in early December in Atlanta.

In 1994, Florida not only had Atlanta in their sights but also had the national championship on their minds. They entered the season as the number one team in the country, but after an early loss to sixth-ranked Auburn and a tie with rival Florida State, the Gators were out of the national title picture. Instead, they would have to settle for another meeting with Alabama in the SEC Championship Game with the opportunity to bring home the conference title. Playing the game at the Georgia Dome for the first time, Florida knocked off the Crimson Tide, 24–23, and in the process became the first back-to-back outright SEC champions since Alabama accomplished the feat in the late 1970s. The Florida Gators were now the class of the SEC. They had only one more hill to climb as they searched for the first national championship in school history.

Steve Spurrier was in the process of building a dynasty at his alma mater, where Florida was finally reaching the potential of which so many thought it was capable. "These Florida Gators were now viewed as winners," Spurrier said years later. "You could see it in the way they carried themselves. The players on the '95 squad felt they were going to win every time they took the field. They competed fiercely in practice, dreamed big, and laughed hard. And they had fun."[26]

The 1995 season saw Florida take another step toward reaching their ultimate goal. Victories in three games against teams ranked in the top 10 (Tennessee, Auburn, and Florida State) and a 34–3 drubbing of Arkansas in the SEC Championship Game helped the Gators complete the first unbeaten and untied regular season in school history. Top-ranked Nebraska awaited Florida in the Fiesta Bowl, with the winner taking home the national championship. The Gators never had a chance, with Spurrier exclaiming, "We ran into a buzz saw."[27] Nebraska scored 29 points in the second quarter alone on their way to a 62–29 victory. Even though many observers consider the 1995 Nebraska squad as the greatest college football team of all time, Spurrier was still looking to make improvements, especially on the defensive side of the ball. He zeroed in on a little-known assistant at Kansas State named Bob Stoops and had to get creative to contact him.

"I began calling out to [Kansas State] Coach Bill Snyder in hopes of obtaining permission to talk to Bob," Spurrier recalled. "After numerous attempts and no return call, I decided to try a different strategy." Realizing that Stoops was friends with one of the coaches on the Florida staff, Lawson Holland, Spurrier picked up the phone and tried again. "The next time I called Bob and the secretary asked who was calling, I told her, 'Tell him it's Lawson Holland,' and finally got through," Spurrier explained. "Bob answered and said, 'Hey Lawson.' I told Bob who it was and then asked him if he was interested in talking about our coordinator job and he said yes. Bob turned out to be one of the best hires I ever made."[28]

Behind quarterback Danny Wuerffel, the Gators Fun 'n' Gun offense rolled to record breaking numbers in 1996 and another string of victories. But after wrapping up another berth in the SEC Championship Game, the Gators fell flat against Florida State in their final regular season game. To reach their goal of a national title, they would need help from other teams around the country and have to take care of their own business. The Gators did their part, beginning in the SEC Championship Game against Alabama. With a 45–30 victory, the Gators won their fourth consecutive conference title, the first such stretch in the SEC since the Crimson Tide won five in a row from 1971 to 1975. A week later, Wuerffel won the Heisman. It was the first time that a former winner coached the current winner of college football's most prestigious award. The only thing standing between Spurrier, Wuerffel, and the Gators and the national championship was none other than Florida State. The rivals would meet in the Sugar Bowl in a rematch, with Florida looking to lay claim as the best team in the country.

Spurrier had complained to the media after their loss in November, telling anyone who would listen that the Florida State players were involved in multiple late hits throughout the game. Seminole athletic director Dave Hart had heard enough, saying, "Give Spurrier a pacifier, put him to bed, and tell him to quit crying."[29] In the end, none of the talking mattered. The Gators hammered Florida State, 52–20, winning the national championship in the process.

It was the second national championship for an SEC team in four years but only the third in the previous 16 years. Things were about to change. The SEC had laid the foundation with expansion, a championship game, and a new TV contract. The national titles were about to become a lot more frequent.

CHAPTER 7

The First Family of the SEC

On Saturday, October 4, 1969, Archie Manning was introduced to the nation, and thanks to the *Lawrence Welk Show*, the junior quarterback would be appearing in prime time. He didn't disappoint in his national TV debut. Manning and the Ole Miss Rebels traveled to Legion Field to face the fifteenth-ranked Alabama Crimson Tide in the first-ever regular season college football game to be broadcast nationally at night. With Major League Baseball playoffs taking place during the day and the *Lawrence Welk Show* occupying its usual spot in the early evening programming window, ABC elected to present their college football telecast beginning at 8:30 p.m. Central Standard Time.

The exploits of Archie Manning had already spread far and wide the year before, when he led the Rebels to a 7–3–1 record, including a win over Alabama. The season culminated in the Liberty Bowl in Memphis. After falling behind, 17–0, to Virginia Tech, Manning orchestrated a masterful comeback, with the Rebels earning a 34–17 victory. The excitement for the prime-time matchup against Alabama was so great that other schools rearranged the start times of their own games to allow for fans to get home in time to watch. Louisville had already printed tickets with the kickoff time listed but insisted on starting their game two hours earlier. The late start tested the patience of some, including the press, who didn't want to have to wait all day in longing anticipation. "The kickoff comes at a late 8:35 p.m., a time established by the television people so the ladies of the nation can see Lawrence Welk while the football fans twiddle their thumbs," a local sports editor opined.[1]

Everything about the game would be worth the wait. A back-and-forth affair, Manning and his Alabama counterpart, Scott Hunter, put on an offensive display that is still talked about at backyard barbecues all over the South. Manning threw for 436 yards on 52 attempts and ran for 104 yards, accounting for five Ole Miss touchdowns. His 540 total yards set an NCAA record that would stand for more than four decades. Hunter threw for 300 yards, including the game-winning touchdown, giving Alabama a 33–32 victory. ABC announcer Chris Schenkel was nearly left speechless, saying, "It was the greatest duel two quarterbacks ever had. You had to be there to believe it."[2]

The same sports editor who was perturbed by the late start had nothing but effusive praise in his column the day following the game. "It took college football 100 years to reach what happened here Saturday night," Jack Doane wrote in the *Montgomery Advertiser*. "Alabama and Mississippi played a football game for the entire nation to see and cherish. Never, never has anything like it been seen before, nor is it likely to be seen again."[3]

Even though Manning found himself on the losing end of this epic battle, he had endeared himself to the Ole Miss faithful forever. He received more than 5,000 pieces of mail the week following the game against Alabama. "I guess that game kind of put me on the map. It jumpstarted what was going to be a pretty eventful season," he modestly understated as he recalled the aftermath years later.[4]

The event also captured the beginning of the legacy of the Manning name being synonymous with SEC football for decades to come. He had been lightly recruited out of high school, with only Mississippi State and Tulane offering him a scholarship in addition to Ole Miss. He also excelled on the baseball field and was drafted by the Atlanta Braves out of high school. But his heart belonged to the gridiron. "My dad loved Ole Miss and he loved [the state of] Mississippi. That really became my dream, to be an Ole Miss quarterback," he said.[5] The opportunity to play for legendary coach John Vaught was too tempting to pass up. He signed with the Rebels and set out from his hometown in the Mississippi Delta to begin his college journey in Oxford.

Ole Miss and Manning bounced back from their loss against Alabama with a win the following week against sixth-ranked Georgia that propelled them to an overall 8–3 record on the season. Manning's junior season was wrapped up on New Year's Day in the Sugar Bowl with a win over third-ranked Arkansas and a fourth-place finish in the Heisman voting.

The final year for Manning in Oxford began with promise as the Rebels opened as the fifth-ranked team in the nation. Again they met Alabama on national TV in their third game of the year, and this time, they dominated the contest, winning easily, 48–23. Even Bear Bryant was impressed. "He could hurt you in more ways than any other quarterback I've seen," the legendary coach said. "Sprinting out, dropping back, throwing while scrambling, and running. His most important assets were leadership and the ability to win close games by the force of his personality and talents."[6]

Unfortunately for Manning and Ole Miss, his senior season ended on a down note. He broke his arm early in the season against Houston, and the Rebels dropped their final three games of the year, including the Gator Bowl against conference rival Auburn. Manning, who was playing with a plastic sleeve to protect his arm, had to come out of the game before its conclusion. "All that scrambling got me," he said. "My wind left me, and those weeks out of action showed up. That old hospital bed never got off my back. As a matter of fact, I felt like it rode down the field with me a couple of times."[7]

Manning wasn't the only Rebel facing health issues in 1970. Head coach John Vaught, in his twenty-third season with the program, was forced to step away after his doctor warned him of having a fatal heart attack if he continued to roam the sidelines. During his tenure, Vaught had taken Ole Miss to heights they had never seen and would not return to again. He presided over six SEC championships, including five in a 10-year period from 1954 through 1963. Ole Miss has not won a conference title under any other coach. His teams laid claim to national championships in 1959, 1960, and 1962. The 1959 squad was named the SEC Team of the Decade by the AP. He led the Rebels to 18 bowl game appearances, including five wins in the Sugar Bowl. His expectations of perfection for his teams had been fostered at a young age by his grandmother on the Texas farm where he was raised. If she didn't like how he mowed the lawn, she would have the task repeated until it was done correctly. "I didn't realize it at the time, but Grandmother taught me the qualities of good leadership," Vaught wrote in his book *Rebel Coach*. "She taught me that something half done was a failure, and that fits my coaching philosophy."[8]

With John Vaught retiring and Archie Manning graduating, Ole Miss football came on hard times in the 1970s. It would be 12 years before another bowl appearance and 16 years before a victory in a bowl game took place. By the late 1980s, Ole Miss had become a middle-of-the-pack team in the SEC, nowhere near the achievements that occurred under Vaught. The lack of success in the Rebel program became even more obtrusive when Archie Manning's son, Peyton, was deciding where to play in college in 1994.

Following college, Archie Manning had a long yet bumpy professional career in the NFL. He played 14 seasons and retired with the seventeenth-most completions in league history, but he also retired with the worst winning percentage of any quarterback making at least 100 starts. He never played on a winning team or made the playoffs. He spent most of his career with the New Orleans Saints, and his family settled in the Crescent City. His second child, Peyton, became one of the most sought-after recruits in SEC history.

Coming out of Isidore Newman High School, Peyton had the attention of every college coach in the country. With both of his parents graduating from Ole Miss, the hope and dream of every Rebel fan was that Peyton would choose to follow the bloodlines and go to school in Oxford. But Tennessee, Michigan, and Florida were also among the finalists vying for the young prodigy. With Ole Miss on probation and the desire to make it on his own, Peyton ultimately settled on Tennessee.

"I thought the Ole Miss thing was weighing really heavy on [Peyton], and he's thinking, 'Alright, if I don't go to Ole Miss, I don't want to play against Ole Miss,'" Archie Manning said after the decision was made. "'I'm getting away from the whole thing.' And I really think [Michigan] was his getaway. At some point, the [Tennessee] coaches convinced him or he convinced himself that by going to the other side of the conference, he wouldn't have to play [Ole Miss] every year."[9]

Peyton felt the weight of the family name before he set foot on an SEC campus. "I know that I'll always have some pressure because my father was a great SEC quarterback and I'll be playing in the SEC. I'll always have to live up to the Manning name."[10]

Once Peyton got to Knoxville, his dedication and single-minded focus on preparation became legendary. So did his competitiveness. Tennessee brought in another freshman quarterback the same year Peyton joined the squad: Branndon Stewart from Texas. Both were content as newcomers to learn the system and work hard enough to fight for a starting job in their second year. But when the incumbent tore his anterior cruciate ligament (ACL) in the first game, their battle for playing time was expedited. Needing to spend as much time as possible in the football facility that fall to learn the offense, both players were expected to meet with the offensive coaches after dinner every night. Coaches had access badges to the building, while the players did not. With the building getting locked up in the evening, the coaches would put a rock in the door to allow Manning and Stewart to enter. However, on multiple occasions when Stewart would arrive, the door would be locked. He would bang and knock on the door, but to no avail, as the meeting rooms were on the third floor, and no one could hear his pleas for help. Years later, Stewart learned what had happened. "Peyton bumped the rock out of the door so I couldn't get in," Stewart said. By the fifth game of his freshman year, Manning was named the starter, a job he wouldn't relinquish until he graduated four years later.[11]

In his first huddle as the quarterback for Tennessee, Manning told his teammates, "I know I'm just a freshman but I can take us down the field." The response from a senior lineman was swift and blunt. "Shut up and call the play."[12] That's exactly what Manning did over his career, and he did it better than just about any quarterback in SEC history. As a sophomore, Manning led the Vols to an 11–1 record and final AP ranking of number two in the country, including a win over Ohio State in the Citrus Bowl. His junior season was filled with similar results: a top 10 ranking and a win in the Citrus Bowl. But with Manning under center, the Vols had failed to beat rival Florida, and they had not won a conference title. Electing to stay in school for one more season rather than turn pro, Manning came back to Tennessee to accomplish both of those feats. He would have to settle for one out of two.

With the switch to division play a few years earlier due to SEC expansion, Tennessee and Florida became fast rivals. Between 1956 and 1989, the two schools had met only seven times. By the time Manning arrived in Knoxville, the game went a long way in determining who won the SEC East. But Tennessee, even with their legacy quarterback, couldn't seem to get over the hump against the Gators. The 1997 game would be no different.

Florida was the defending national champs and ranked number one in the country entering the 1997 matchup. The Vols were ranked fourth, marking the second year in a row the teams would face off as top five teams. In front of a national TV audience on CBS, the Gators jumped out to a 14–0 lead and never looked back on their way to a 33–20 victory. It was the fifth consecutive win for Florida over the Vols. Manning was devastated but maintained a healthy view of the bigger picture. "I'm disappointed, but I didn't come back just for this game," he said after the defeat. "There is a lot of football to be played. I'm disappointed for our fans, our coaches and for our seniors, who have never beaten Florida. I needed to play extremely well to win this ball game and I didn't do that."[13]

Two weeks later, Manning and Tennessee faced thirteenth-ranked Georgia. Another loss would knock the Vols out of the hunt for the Eastern Division title completely. In front of 106,000 fans and millions watching across the country on CBS, Manning lived up to the moment. He completed 31 of 40 passes for 343 yards and four touchdowns as Tennessee ran away with a 38–13 win, their seventh straight in the series. That same Saturday, Florida was upset by LSU, giving life to the Vols. One more loss by the Gators and Tennessee would control their own destiny for the SEC Eastern Division title. The third Saturday in October would present their next challenge.

Alabama and Tennessee began playing on the third Saturday in October 1928, and by 1939, it became recognized as the name of the rivalry. "You never know what a football player is made of until he plays Alabama," legendary Tennessee coach Robert Neyland once famously said. "Tennessee [players] don't deserve citizenship papers until they have survived an Alabama game." As much as Manning struggled against Florida, he dominated the Crimson Tide over his college career, leading the Vols to a victory in the rivalry in his final three seasons in Knoxville. "We all remember the things we do in the Alabama game," former Vols coach Johnny Majors said.[14] For the rest of his life, Peyton Manning would have nothing but fond memories of his battles against the Tide.

With wins over Alabama and Georgia, the Vols had their most difficult opponents out of the way. On November 1, they defeated South Carolina and received a gift courtesy of the Bulldogs. Florida was upset by Georgia, paving the way for Tennessee and Peyton Manning to finally have their shot at the SEC Championship. Fighting a reputation that winning in big games was beyond the reach of both Manning and the Tennessee program, the Vols were in search of their first outright SEC title since 1969. Their opponent in the Georgia Dome would be eleventh-ranked Auburn, with both schools making their first appearance in the conference title game. Tennessee and Auburn played every year from 1956 through the 1991 season. The move to divisional play ended the annual affair, and they had not faced each other since the SEC expanded. They would meet only 10 times over the next 25 years after facing off in the 1997 title game.

Leading up to the game, Manning was pestered by reporters about the Heisman, which would be awarded a week later. "People think that I need this award, and that really isn't true," he said. "I was never taught to play for individual awards. I think about it, because people ask me about it every day. But it doesn't stay on my mind very long. It doesn't keep me awake at night."[15] He also maintained that the pressure of the family name wasn't bothering him either. "My Dad has never mentioned [the Heisman] to me one time in my life," he said. "He was, I guess, the favorite at the end of [his senior season] and got hurt. But it's never bothered him one day in his life. We'll take it; but we don't need it."

Tennessee started slowly in the title game, finding themselves in a 20–7 hole early in the second quarter to Auburn. Even though they committed six turnovers, Manning and the Vols put together a rally that culminated with a 73-yard touchdown pass in the fourth quarter to give them a 30–29 victory. Destiny had finally been fulfilled, and they were champions of the SEC at last. Manning put an exclamation point on the outcome as he climbed the ladder posted in front of the Tennessee band and led the Vol faithful in a rousing rendition of "Rocky Top," the venerable fight song at the school. "This is why you play college football," Manning said after the game.[16]

Peyton Manning finished second in the Heisman voting to Michigan defensive back Charles Woodson in results that are controversial to this day. Manning became only the fourth quarterback in NCAA history to pass for more than 11,000 yards. Woodson was the first and only defensive player to win the award. While Manning never won the Heisman or a national championship, he did become the first individual star of CBS's coverage of the SEC. His junior year coincided with the inaugural season of the long-term contract that CBS signed with the conference. Manning and Tennessee would appear on the network 10 times over his final two years playing college football, gaining more exposure than anyone else in the SEC. Peyton would not be the last Manning to play under center in the SEC. The powerful combination of network television and the SEC was only beginning.

* * *

When Peyton Manning graduated from high school in New Orleans, he left a message on his locker "The best is yet to come." It was a subtle reference to his brother Elisha, who was five years younger and would be following in his footsteps as a highly recruited quarterback in the South. However, Eli, as he would be known, did not want to come after Peyton and do things exactly the same way his older brother did it. "Peyton is extraneously outgoing, outspoken and never met a microphone he didn't like," Ken Trahan, who has covered sports in New Orleans for decades, said. "Eli's nickname was 'Easy.' He was the opposite [of Peyton]. Eli was very low-key. His [college] recruitment was much like his persona. It certainly didn't attract the attention that Peyton's did. There's only one first."[17]

As a high school quarterback, Eli broke many of the records that Peyton had set years earlier, and he was a highly sought-after prospect by every major football power in the fall of 1998. David Cutcliffe, the offensive coordinator at Tennessee, had forged a strong bond with the Manning family while Peyton was in Knoxville. He was given the task by Phil Fulmer to recruit Eli and convince him to play for the Vols just like his older brother did. But Eli had no interest in playing for Tennessee, consistently telling Cutcliffe that he wanted to establish his own path separate from his brother. Texas, Virginia, and Ole Miss were the final three schools Eli had narrowed his options down to, with Ole Miss seen as a long shot. That's when fate intervened, and the Rebels jumped to the front of the line.

Following the 1998 season, when Tennessee captured the national title, Ole Miss head coach Tommy Tuberville announced that he was leaving for Auburn. Archie Manning said that Tuberville called Eli only one time during the recruitment. "Eli was kind of wondering" how much he was wanted by Ole Miss, Archie said.[18] The Rebels turned to Cutcliffe to take over the program in Oxford. Cutcliffe picked up the phone and made his first call to a recruit as the head coach for Ole Miss. "All right, Eli, all bets are off," he said. "You're going to Ole Miss."[19]

Eli announced his intentions to play for Ole Miss at the end of his senior football season. At the press conference, he insisted that the pressure wouldn't be a problem. "That was 30 years ago [when Archie played at Ole Miss]; I think wherever I would have gone, there would have been pressure," he said. "I've just got to live up to it. I've got to accept that and not worry about it. I'm going to work hard and do all I can to be the best quarterback I can be."[20]

Cutcliffe wanted to be sure that Eli knew what he was getting into by choosing to go to the school his father had played for. "Eli looked for a lot of different things. What his life was going to be like, who his friends were going to be," Cutcliffe said. "He just has a brother who is the best player in the Southeastern Conference and he's willing to follow a dad who's the speed limit on campus. His jersey number is the miles-per-hour on campus. Arguably the best player in Ole Miss history. You're willing to follow that?"[21]

Eli lived up to the hype at Ole Miss. He became the starting quarterback in 2001, the beginning of his sophomore year. He helped the Rebels to a 7–4 record, including a win over Alabama for the first time since 1988 and only the second time in 25 years. His junior season also concluded with seven wins, including a victory over Nebraska in the Independence Bowl. The highlight of the year came when they upset sixth-ranked Florida in Oxford. Ole Miss sports information director Langston Rogers named it one of the five biggest wins in program history. Eli also did something that Peyton couldn't do and that Archie didn't have the opportunity to do: beat the Gators. Peyton was 0–4 against Florida during his time at Tennessee. Ole Miss never faced the Gators while Archie played for the Rebels. The game also marked the first appearance for Eli on CBS. Ole Miss would be selected three more times by the network during Eli's collegiate career, doubling the number of appearances they had previously.

The 2003 season, Eli's final year in college, got off to a rocky start, as Ole Miss dropped two of their first four games. They got on track in their fifth game of the year, when they upset Florida again, this time in the Swamp, with Archie watching from the stands. "[My dad] claimed after Peyton left [college] that he'd never come back to Gainesville or The Swamp," Eli said after the win. "So he had one last trip and he got to end it on a good one."[22] It was the beginning of a six-game winning streak for the Rebels, including victories over Alabama and Auburn in the same season for the first time ever. At 8–2 and unbeaten in conference play, Ole Miss hosted LSU and Nick Saban for the right to represent the SEC West in the title game in Atlanta. The Rebels, looking for their first conference championship since 1962, fell short, losing to the eventual national champions, 17–14. They bounced back the following week to defeat their rival, Mississippi State, and earn a berth in the Cotton Bowl, where they beat Oklahoma State, 31–28. It was the first 10-win season for Ole Miss since 1971.

The latest Manning chapter in the SEC storybook had come to an end. Eli was named SEC Offensive Player of the Year and finished third in the Heisman voting. It was all more than Archie had ever bargained for. "We just tried to raise kids . . . good kids and have a good family,"

Archie said years later. "I don't like the perception that it was a plan. That because I was an NFL quarterback for a while, and I've got these boys and I'm going to mold them into being NFL quarterbacks. Not so. You might can do that, and they might can be an NFL quarterback, but I'm not sure you're going to have a good father-son relationship, and that's what I wanted."[23]

* * *

Major college football had a long and strange history of crowning a national champion. At the conclusion of each season, media members would cast votes in one poll, biased coaches would do the same in another, and a handful of computer algorithms would bypass humans altogether to name their own title winner. As time went on, not only did the sport refuse to put together a playoff, but it also stuck to traditional conference bowl tie-ins that often precluded the top two teams from meeting at the end of the season. This practice often resulted in a "split" national champion, where the media and coaches selected different teams to finish number one. This scenario played out in 1978 with an SEC team when Alabama was named the champion by the media but USC was voted number one by the coaches. Because the SEC champion was contractually obligated to play in the Sugar Bowl and USC faced the same commitment through the Pac-10 to compete in the Rose Bowl, they could not meet and settle it on the field. A split national championship occurred 10 times between 1954 and 1997. Prior to 1997, the number one and number two teams in the country had met only eight times in a bowl game. Roy Kramer had seen enough.

Kramer began having conversations with other conference commissioners to gauge interest in combining forces and creating a system that would produce a matchup with the two top-ranked teams in a bowl game at the end of the season. Agreements among some conferences prior to 1998 had been in effect. The Bowl Coalition and Bowl Alliance existed from 1992 to 1997, but both were missing the Big Ten and Pac-10, who refused to part ways with their tradition of sending conference champions to the Rose Bowl. Kramer worked hard on his conference commissioner colleagues.

"I thought we needed to do some things, particularly to put together some better matchups in some of our bowl games, to find a way to increase the excitement," Kramer said. "The NFL was so strong and so big that we needed to find ways to increase the interest in the college game."[24]

Not only did Kramer have to convince the Big Ten and Pac-10 to participate, but he also had to get the blessing of the "Granddaddy of Them All," the Rose Bowl. "The greatest fear of the Rose Bowl people was that in a given year the Big Ten and Pac-10 champs would finish 1–2 in the BCS and that year the national championship would be played in another bowl like the Sugar," Kramer said. "We researched it, and it had only happened one time in 50 years that those leagues were Nos. 1–2 nationally."[25]

Jim Delany, the Big Ten commissioner, finally came around to the idea when he was ensured that the new system would be very similar to what college football had known for decades. "It was important to us to have a national championship within the context of the traditional bowl system," Delany said. "We thought this was an important thing, to make the bowl system healthier, because we don't want an NFL-style playoff. But we understood America's appetite for a 1–2 game."[26] He also realized it would be damaging to his conference members if they continued to be on the outside looking in. "It came to the point where it was the right thing to do for the Big Ten and the right thing for college football. It wasn't healthy for the Big Ten to be separated."[27]

Beginning with the 1998 season, the BCS would use a combination of media, coach, and computer polls to match the two top teams in a bowl game. The site would rotate each year among the Rose, Sugar, Orange, and Fiesta bowls. The SEC, Big Ten, Big 12, ACC, Pac-10, and Big East were the conferences that initially agreed to participate. The BCS was immediately met with apprehension and skepticism from fans and the media alike. At the 1998 SEC Media Days, with Kramer sitting in the back of the room, Steve Spurrier unloaded as only he could. "I think [the BCS is] so good they ought to take it to basketball, baseball, tennis, golf—make 'em all go through it," he said sarcastically. "I've just never understood why we're the only sport in the world without a playoff

system. Can't figure that out. Why we don't get 16 teams and start playing at the end of the season just amazes me, but we keep doing it the
old way."[28] Kramer held strong in the face of the criticism and pushed
forward building out the administration of the new-look postseason for
college football.

With Kramer bringing computer analysis into the model, he contacted Jeff Sagarin, a sports statistician who had been publishing his
college football rankings in *USA Today* beginning in 1985. "I got a
phone call from Roy Kramer," Sagarin said. "He had met me initially in
1988 during the Dodgers-Oakland A's World Series. He remembered
me. He called me and said, 'Hey, we're doing this thing called the BCS,
do you want to be a part of it? We're going to have a computer rating.' I
said, 'Yeah, sure, be happy to.'"[29]

Kramer and Sagarin developed a love–hate relationship as the initial
season progressed. The rankings would get released each week, and the
media would reach out to Sagarin to get his opinion. "Each week I'd get
a call from Roy and the first 30 seconds would be Roy screaming at me
to keep my mouth shut," Sagarin said. "The media would be going to him
saying, 'Did you hear what Sagarin said?' Roy would say, 'You're killing
me.' But he couldn't keep it up. He'd start laughing and we'd have a great
conversation."[30]

Because the BCS was Kramer's creation, the tabulations each week
originated with him. "It was run out of [the SEC] office," conference
media relations director Charles Bloom said. "On Sunday, the numbers
would come into our office. I would do mine handwritten. Sometimes
I would get an email from the commissioner at 3 a.m. We were heavily
invested, time-wise."[31] Every Sunday during that first season, Kramer
and Bloom would set up at the kitchen table in their homes with dozens
of pages full of notes and data while on the phone with each other. As
the 1998 season progressed, the SEC suddenly found itself in a sticky
situation with a member institution that was surprisingly undefeated and
making a run at the very first BCS National Championship.

Without Peyton Manning under center, many expected Tennessee
to take a step back after he graduated. But coach Phil Fulmer had built
a program that was much more than just their legacy quarterback. The

1998 Vols, behind new signal-caller Tee Martin, began the year ranked tenth in the country. In the second game of the season, they finally got over the hump against Florida, beating the Gators for the first time in six years and only the third time since 1976. From that point, they went on a tear, crushing seventh-ranked Georgia and squeaking by tenth-ranked Arkansas on their way to an unbeaten record as they prepared for the SEC Championship Game against twenty-third-ranked Mississippi State. Tennessee had the top spot in the BCS polls, and the prevailing sentiment was that all they needed to clinch a berth in the inaugural BCS Championship Game was to defeat the Bulldogs in Atlanta. But UCLA and Kansas State also entered the final weekend without a loss, and Sagarin didn't adhere to popular opinion.

A reporter contacted Sagarin looking for an opinion on which team would be left out of the title game should all three win their final contest. Sagarin answered the question with brutal honesty. "I like Kansas State's chances but I'm starting to feel uncomfortable about Tennessee," he said. "If all three win, Tennessee's out." Kramer was not pleased when he heard the remark. "Roy called me and told me I needed to keep my mouth shut."

"It made for a tense week at the office," Charles Bloom said. "The first year of the BCS system [that the SEC] developed, and an undefeated team from our conference was about to get left out."[32]

As it turned out, Kramer and his BCS team within the SEC office didn't have to worry. After falling behind, 14–10, in the fourth quarter, Tennessee scored two quick touchdowns on their way to a 24–14 win over Mississippi State in the SEC Championship Game. Tennessee captured their second consecutive SEC title, the first time the Vols had won back-to-back outright conference championships since their three-peat in 1938–1940 under Robert Neyland. Both UCLA and Kansas State lost that day, making the Vols the easy and obvious number one team in the country and sending them to the inaugural BCS Championship Game, hosted by the Fiesta Bowl in Arizona. Their opponent in the desert would be a one-loss Florida State team that was on a 10-game winning streak.

Even though Tennessee was the higher-ranked team, they entered their matchup against Florida State as the underdog. Ready to claim his moment in history, Tee Martin was anxious to prove that the Vols were bigger than any one player. Days before the game, he told reporters that "it was like we didn't exist at the university for a couple of years." Florida State would find out not only that Martin did exist but also that he was not afraid of his moment on the big stage. Teammate Al Wilson explained, "I've never seen Tee Martin nervous and I think that's one of his biggest attributes. He's always relaxed."[33]

The first score in a BCS title game was a touchdown pass Martin threw early in the second quarter as Tennessee opened with a 7–0 lead. That was followed by a 54-yard pick-six by Volunteer defensive back Dwayne Goodrich. Florida State never recovered. Receiver Peerless Price had four catches for 199 yards and scored the final touchdown to help Tennessee earn the 23–14 victory over the Seminoles. After the game, Martin not only was elated but also gave an insight into his motivation, saying, "It feels great. We had to prove to everybody we were the number one team in the nation. All the adversity we faced, all the guys that went to the NFL last year, all the shoes we had to fill. We had a chip on our shoulders. We won all our games, we were 12–0 and we still didn't get our respect."[34]

For Tennessee head coach Phil Fulmer, the championship was a dream come true. The former Volunteer offensive lineman had helped his alma mater accomplish something that had not happened for decades in Knoxville. "It's been 47 years since Tennessee has brought one of these home," he declared as he embraced the trophy after the win. "It wasn't always pretty, it wasn't always perfect, but we found a way to get it done."[35] Not only had Tennessee won their first national title since 1951, but the SEC had also captured the very first national championship in the BCS era. It also represented the third and final title for the SEC in the 1990s. At the time, the world of college football didn't put too much meaning behind the momentum that the conference was beginning to build. Schools outside the SEC would have only a few years left before the conference would begin to put a stranglehold on national championships. Two coaches with northern roots were about to enter the picture and change everything both inside and outside the conference.

* * *

When the SEC broke rank with the CFA in 1996 to sign an exclusive contract with CBS, it was hardly the obvious move to make. Commissioner Roy Kramer and the 12 member schools in the conference were betting that the increased exposure offered by their new network television partner would pay dividends down the road. Toward the end of their first season together, the TV ratings for the SEC on CBS were so paltry that ABC openly gloated. "This wasn't rocket science to forecast," David Downs, the senior vice president of ABC Sports, said at the time. "We had a good idea of what CBS would program. I don't think CBS can ever beat us."[36]

Even the mighty *New York Times* shared their opinion of the new SEC/CBS partnership. After a national broadcast of Tennessee versus Kentucky in 1996 failed to get even 25 percent of the viewers of ABC's regional coverage, a *Times* headline blared, "CBS Being Beaten by ABC and Geography." The accompanying article proclaimed, "You can't say CBS wasn't warned that its college football mix of Big East and Southeastern Conference games was geographically flawed. So far this season, its 3.3 national Nielsen rating is 45 percent below ABC's 4.8."[37]

Kramer remained calm and confident, as did his associates at CBS, regarding the future of the SEC as the featured conference on network television. With Florida winning the national championship in 1996 and prominent players such as Peyton Manning at Tennessee, CBS quickly doubled down on their relationship with the conference. A full three years before their current deal was set to expire, CBS and the SEC came to an agreement in February 1998 for a new contract that would go into effect in 2001 and continue through the 2008 season. "[The new contract] reflects the value of SEC football and basketball, solidifies CBS' position as the network of college sports and signals a strong commitment by CBS Sports to feature the best college football as a cornerstone of fall programming well into the 21st century," CBS vice president Mike Aresco said.[38]

Only a month earlier, in January 1996, CBS announced that they were back in business with the NFL as they picked up the American

Football Conference (AFC) package from NBC. "The negative impact [of losing the NFL] was so severe that CBS went to the NFL and said, 'Name your price and we'll pay whatever to get a package,'" said Neal Pilson, the former president of CBS Sports. "We lost affiliates, ratings, the male audience and a lot of sports sponsorships. But when CBS got the NFL back, everything picked up again."[39]

The possibility to use the NFL audience to build awareness for the SEC games was too promising to pass up for the CBS executives. "No one else would have had a chance to negotiate [with the SEC] until 2000, but the longer you wait, the more variables can enter the equation," Aresco said. "The SEC football package is even more viable because of the strategic cross-promotion opportunities with the NFL. When we're doing [a game] on a Sunday afternoon, we'll be able to say to that audience, 'Don't forget, we've got Tennessee-Florida coming.'"[40]

Kramer also continued to partner with ESPN for games on Saturday night during prime time as well as in the early TV window at noon Eastern Standard Time. The new contracts with CBS and ESPN would more than double the previous deal and bring the conference more than $50 million per season, vaulting the SEC ahead of rival conferences, such as the Big Ten and Pac-10. Three years later, in 2001, CBS finally became home to the SEC Championship Game as well, taking the rights over from ABC by doubling the fees to more than $9 million per year. The most compelling SEC game was broadcast to the nation every week at 3:30 Eastern Standard Time on CBS, and the regular season would conclude with the SEC Championship Game on CBS. The Tiffany Network was all in on SEC football.

"[The SEC] is a good investment for us for a lot of reasons," Mike Aresco said. "It brings in viewers that advertisers covet, a younger demographic. We are bringing in more and more female viewers. It works well for the advertisers and the affiliates. It fills a nice niche for us, and the SEC is the most important conference relationship. It is the only conference that has a national football deal, and we found that we made a leap of faith which was also a calculated risk that doing a one-conference deal would work both economically and with the ratings."[41]

Roy Kramer had taken over as commissioner of the SEC in 1990 and deftly guided the conference to unforeseen heights. From leading the way on expansion to negotiating television contracts and creating the BCS, collegiate sports had never seen someone like Kramer. He was born in 1929 in Maryville, Tennessee; played football at Maryville College; and became a lieutenant in the NATO command in Europe. Following his military career, he coached high school football, then was the head coach at Central Michigan from 1967 to 1977. In 1974, he led his team to the Division II national championship and was named national coach of the year. He moved into administration when he was named the athletic director at Vanderbilt in 1978, thus beginning his foray into the SEC. In the spring of 2002 at 72 years old, Kramer announced that he was retiring.

In 1990, Kramer's first year on the job, the SEC distributed $16.3 million to their member institutions. By the time Kramer was riding off into the sunset 12 years later, the conference was sharing almost $95 million among the schools. "He elevated this conference from a very fine conference to in my opinion, the nation's finest," Florida athletic director Jeremy Foley said after hearing the news of the retirement. "He will be tremendously missed but his legacy will be here forever."[42] For his part, Kramer wasn't worried about the future of the conference. "This conference was a great conference before I ever got here," he said. "This conference will be a great conference after Roy Kramer is gone. It has been a great ride over these 12 years."[43]

On July 2, 2002, Mike Slive was named the seventh commissioner of the SEC. The Dartmouth graduate and Chicago resident had been the commissioner of Conference USA since 1995. Prior to becoming involved in college athletics, Slive had been a lawyer in Chicago and a judge in New Hampshire. Dr. John White, chancellor of the University of Arkansas and president of the SEC, said of Slive, "We think that Mike will build on the success that the SEC enjoyed under Roy Kramer. Mike is familiar with the league and he has been active on NCAA committees. He will bring the same level of commitment to excellence that Commissioner Kramer has done the past 12 years. We're excited about what Mike will be able to do working with the presidents and chancellors, athletics directors and coaches of the SEC in the league's continuing efforts to be the premier athletic conference in the nation."[44]

CHAPTER 8

Nick and Urban

TIGER STADIUM ON THE LSU CAMPUS HASN'T ALWAYS BEEN KNOWN AS "Death Valley," filled with more than 100,000 passionate fans. The enthusiasm and zest for their football team goes back more than 100 years. In 1928, T. P. "Skipper" Heard caught wind that LSU president James Smith wanted to spend $250,000 to build much-needed dormitories on campus. Heard, who at the time was the LSU graduate manager for the football team and would later become the athletic director, came up with a creative idea that could happen only in SEC country. He managed to gain the attention of Smith and convince him to use the funds to build the new dorms into a refurbished Tiger Stadium. Amazingly, the school president loved the idea, and they moved forward with construction. The stands were extended on both sidelines into the end zones, in the process adding 10,000 seats to the stadium and creating living quarters underneath the bleachers, with windows that faced the street. Heard remained practical when the project was completed. "What it meant was, for $250,000, the president got his dormitories and we increased the seating capacity," he said. The dorms housed 1,500 students and remained in use for more than 50 years, including the 1986 season, when the football team lived there while their dorms were under construction.[1]

Playing in their remodeled stadium with dorm rooms beneath the seats, LSU won the SEC title in 1935 and 1936 under coach Bernie Moore, who would later become the second commissioner of the fledgling conference. Appearances in the Sugar Bowl followed both of those campaigns, but it would be 25 years before the next conference championship. From 1938 through the 1954 season, the Tigers finished in the top half of the SEC only two times. A coaching change was made prior to the 1955 season, as Paul Dietzel, a former assistant coach for Bear Bryant at Kentucky, was brought in to lead the program. The fortunes of LSU football really began to change when a local Baton Rouge kid named Billy Cannon showed up on campus.

Cannon had offers to play college football from institutions all over the South, including powerhouse Ole Miss. The Rebels won back-to-back SEC titles when Cannon was a junior and senior in high school, but he elected to attend LSU. Staying close to home factored into his decision, but the Tigers also guaranteed a summer job for Cannon, the only program willing to make such a commitment to the star recruit. LSU battled their way to a 5–5 record in 1957, Cannon's sophomore year, which was seen as a success considering that they were picked to finish last in the conference. Sharing the backfield with future Green Bay Packer Jim Taylor, Cannon was named second-team all-conference.

LSU began the 1958 season unranked but quickly gained national attention after wins in their first four games, including defeating Alabama in Bear Bryant's debut as head coach of the Crimson Tide. "Baton Rouge happens to be the worst place in the world to be a visiting team," Bryant said years later. "It's a dugout arena, and you get all of that noise. It's like being inside a drum."[2] After throttling Miami, 41–0, the Tigers jumped into the AP top 10 and solidified their status as a national title contender when they beat sixth-ranked Ole Miss, 14–0. LSU remained unbeaten and held the top spot in the AP poll heading into their final game with Tulane and clinched the national championship with a 62–0 beatdown of their rival. It was the first official national title for LSU and their first season to go undefeated since 1908. Cannon was named a unanimous all-American and the UPI national player of the year.

With Cannon returning for his senior season, LSU began the 1959 campaign ranked number one in the country. The Tigers continued their winning ways with victories in their first six games of the season and then welcomed third-ranked Ole Miss to Baton Rouge on Halloween on a foggy, almost mystical night at Tiger Stadium. Trailing, 3–0, late in the fourth quarter, LSU forced the Rebels to punt on their own 42-yard line. Waiting calmly deep in his own territory was Billy Cannon. Ole Miss coach John Vaught told his punter to kick the ball out of bounds and keep the ball out of Cannon's hands. The kick stayed in the field of play, bouncing before Cannon plucked it out of the air. Fielding the ball on the 11-yard line, Cannon darted up the sideline. At the 20-yard line, he was met with a group of Rebel defenders, but he broke six tackles to get through the scrum, pulling away from the punter to score the decisive touchdown.

Coach Paul Dietzel felt a variety of emotions during the spectacular play. "I watched the ball bounce down by the ten, and I kept saying 'no, Billy, no!'" he said, recounting what happened. "Then it became 'go, Billy, go!' You have to understand, it was a hot, muggy night and late in the game. The players on both teams were exhausted, but not Billy. He was so strong, so fast, he basically ran through the whole team."[3]

Watching the punt return unfold on the opposite sideline, coach Vaught later cracked, "Outside of the Louisiana Purchase in 1803, many Cajuns consider Billy Cannon's run the greatest event in state history."[4] The run not only clinched the victory for LSU but also sealed the Heisman for Billy Cannon, who became only the second player from the SEC to bring home the most prestigious individual award in college football. The following weekend, LSU was not only unbeaten heading into their matchup against Tennessee but also yet to give up a touchdown all season. The game changed when the Vols returned an interception 59 yards for a score, and the Tigers were unable to recover. They lost, 14–13, ending their bid for consecutive conference and national championships. Regardless, the 1958 and '59 LSU squads, led by Billy Cannon, remain etched in the lore of LSU football forever.

Paul Dietzel stepped down as the LSU coach following the 1961 season to take over at Army, and the Tiger faithful would be forced to endure countless ups and downs as the years rolled by. From 1959 through the 2000 season, LSU would claim only two outright SEC championships and cycle through seven different head coaches. But the lack of a consistent winner didn't dampen the passion that Tiger fans held for their program. In a 1988 game against fourth-ranked Auburn, LSU scored a go-ahead touchdown with less than two minutes on the clock that put the crowd into such a frenzy that the seismograph at the LSU Department of Geology registered that an earthquake had occurred. By the late 1990s, the program had stalled, and LSU decided to look northward for a coach who could re-create the glory years of Billy Cannon.

Nick Saban was born and raised in West Virginia, played college football at Kent State in Ohio, and, outside of a short stint as an assistant with the Houston Oilers, had spent his entire coaching career in northern outposts. From 1995 to 1999, Saban was the head coach at Michigan State and had steadily built the Spartans into winners. By the 1999 season, Saban had his machine clicking, with Michigan State rolling to a 9–2 record and a Citrus Bowl appearance. In November 1999, LSU knew that they would be moving on from their current head coach at season's end and began the search for a new leader, but Saban was not at the top of their list. Initially, the LSU brass was attracted to Miami Hurricanes coach Butch Davis and offered him the job. While intrigued at first, after four days of thinking it over, Davis turned down the offer. Explaining his decision to LSU athletic director Joe Dean, Davis said, "I can win this league I'm in now [the ACC]. That league you're in is a monster."[5] Losing out on Davis, Dean moved on to other candidates, but none of the other prospects presented enough of a compelling case to move forward with an offer.

As the process dragged on, LSU identified Florida State offensive coordinator Mark Richt as a possible target. But just as they were getting ready to set up a meeting with him, they were put in contact with Jimmy Sexton, the agent for Nick Saban. Sexton convinced Dean to give Saban an interview, and Dean agreed. The meeting took place at Sexton's house outside of Memphis on a chilly Saturday afternoon, as Dean, along with LSU chancellor Mark Emmert, settled in to spend some time with Saban. It was a meeting that would alter the history of LSU and the SEC.

Saban blew the LSU contingent away with his preparation for the meeting and vision for the program. "He had done extraordinary research and given really deep thought to what was possible at LSU," Emmert described. "LSU had not won a championship in fifty years, and people were still talking about Billy Cannon's run on Halloween like it happened the day before. It had been a long time since the last national championship. Nick recognized that Louisiana led the nation in NFL players per capita, and he had a plan to win a championship."[6]

Even before the meeting concluded, the LSU administrators identified Saban as the man who could bring championships to Baton Rouge. They offered him the job on the spot, with a total compensation package of $1.2 million. The contract would make Saban the third-highest-paid coach in the country and the SEC behind Steve Spurrier at Florida and Phillip Fulmer at Tennessee. Saban accepted the position, and in the process, LSU let everyone in the SEC and beyond know that they were serious about becoming one of the premier programs in the country.

At the press conference announcing Nick Saban as the new head coach, LSU chancellor Mark Emmert didn't hide from their ambitions, saying, "Simply put, success in LSU football is essential for the success of Louisiana State University."[7] Saban embraced the challenge ahead of him, telling the media, "I think that we should always be in the Top 25. And I certainly think that we want to win our conference and play in the championship game. And if you do that, you're very close to being one of the top teams in the country."[8]

In his first season patrolling the sidelines at LSU, Nick Saban got right to work. He brought in offensive coordinator Jimbo Fisher from Cincinnati and later hired 32-year-old Will Muschamp to run the defense. The Tigers had a combined record in SEC games of 3–13 the two years before Saban showed up. But in 2000, Saban got the program back on track with a 7–4 record and a win in the Peach Bowl. He pushed LSU to take an even bigger step in his second season in 2001 with a little help from some conference foes. Even though the Tigers had the same SEC record of 5–3 as they did the year before, they qualified for their first-ever appearance in the conference championship game thanks to Auburn losing to Alabama on the final Saturday in November. Nick Saban's early success in turning the program around caught the LSU administration off guard. "We didn't even know how to distribute tickets for the [2001] SEC championship game," said Skip Bertman, the LSU athletic director at the time. "My [predecessor] and others in the [LSU athletic] department didn't think we could ever win the SEC [West]."[9]

Looking for their first outright SEC championship in 15 years, LSU faced second-ranked and heavily favored Tennessee in Atlanta. Down, 17–10, at halftime, the Tigers exploded in the second half for 21 points and upset Tennessee, 31–20, to win the SEC. The loss knocked the Vols from playing in the BCS Championship Game and vaulted LSU into their first Sugar Bowl since 1987. In just his second season, Nick Saban had delivered a championship.

The 2002 season didn't feature a repeat title for LSU. The Tigers began the year with a loss to Virginia Tech and finished the season with an 8–4 record. They earned a trip to the Cotton Bowl for the first time since 1966, losing to ninth-ranked Texas, 35–20. Saban had been in Baton Rouge four seasons, with a record of 26–12 as the LSU head coach. With only one SEC title to his credit and an average of three losses per season, not many observers recognized that Saban was setting up the program for a run at the national championship in his fifth season on the job at LSU.

LSU began the 2003 campaign ranked fourteenth in the AP poll, which placed the Tigers behind fellow SEC foes Auburn (sixth), Georgia (eleventh), and Tennessee (twelfth). But after three easy wins to open the season, LSU had the opportunity to seize control of their own destiny in a matchup with Georgia in Baton Rouge. Rather than following LSU tradition and playing the game at night, the game was selected by CBS to kick off in the afternoon for the entire nation to view. In a battle that *Sports Illustrated* later proclaimed was the "single greatest day game in the history of Tiger Stadium," LSU outlasted Georgia, 17–10, scoring a late touchdown to seal the victory. LSU quarterback Matt Mauck recognized the importance of the win. "That Georgia game put LSU on the map," he said. "It was our coming-out party."[10]

With the win over Georgia, the Tigers rose to number six in the polls but stumbled at home two weeks later against unranked Florida. Another loss would not only knock LSU out of the SEC race but also eliminate them from national title contention. Following the defeat to the Gators, LSU rattled off four straight wins, including a 27–3 thrashing of Alabama, that pushed them to number three in the BCS poll. Now sitting at 9–1, the Tigers traveled to fifteenth-ranked Ole Miss for a showdown against Eli Manning that would determine the SEC Western Division title. From 1965 through the 1987 season, Ole Miss hosted LSU in Jackson, Mississippi, rather than at their on-campus stadium in Oxford. Not until Ole Miss expanded Vaught-Hemingway Stadium to a capacity larger than the stadium in Jackson did they begin to host opponents such as LSU. In front of the largest crowd to ever watch a football game in Oxford, LSU knocked off the Rebels, 17–14. LSU was heading to their second SEC Championship Game. Awaiting the Tigers in Atlanta: a rematch with Georgia and a possible berth in the BCS title game with a win.

By 2003, the BCS was in its sixth year of existence as it attempted to match the top two teams in the country in one of four bowl games at the conclusion of the regular season. Heading into the championship games the first weekend in December, Oklahoma was unbeaten and ranked number one in the BCS poll. USC came in with only one loss, which was early in the season at California in triple overtime. LSU, also with just one defeat, was ranked third. The Tigers would need to get past Georgia and then hope for one of the teams ahead of them to lose if they wanted a shot at their first national championship since 1957. The BCS wanted to avoid controversy and was longing for Oklahoma to win and for either USC or LSU to lose. Above all else, the BCS was hoping to steer clear of the nightmare scenario of having three one-loss teams when everything was settled.

LSU was determined to do everything in their power to get an opportunity to play for the national title and never really gave Georgia any hope of winning the SEC in their highly anticipated rematch. Late in the first quarter, with no score in the game, Tiger running back Justin Vincent took a pitch in the backfield and sprinted down the sideline for an 87-yard touchdown. LSU forced the Bulldogs to punt on the ensuing possession, but the Georgia punter mishandled the snap and was tackled in the end zone. The rout was on, and LSU never looked back on their way to a 34–13 win. Afterward, Georgia coach Mark Richt was speechless. "Not much to say. We got whipped."[11]

Earlier in the day, USC defeated Oregon State, but in the Big 12 Championship Game, Oklahoma was shocked by Kansas State, losing to the Wildcats, 35–7. The dreaded outcome that the BCS was desperate to avoid was now a reality. While Saban pleaded his case to have LSU participate in the championship game, he also took responsibility. "We have one loss this season that, if we hadn't lost that game, we wouldn't have a problem right now," he said. "We're still responsible for where we are and what's happened." [2] Ultimately, the BCS system that Roy Kramer helped create placed Oklahoma first and LSU second. It was USC that was left out, even though they occupied the number one spot in the AP poll. Nick Saban had led LSU to its second SEC title in three years and was now on the cusp of bringing a national championship back to Baton Rouge.

Scheduled on January 4, 2004, the BCS Championship Game was set for the Sugar Bowl in New Orleans, right down the road from the LSU campus. It was essentially a home game for the Tigers. Even though Oklahoma was quarterbacked by Heisman winner Jason White and averaged 45 points per game during the season, the Sooners were unable to find any rhythm on offense. The LSU defense harassed White all night long, sacking him seven times and holding him to only 102 yards passing in the game. With a final score of 21–14, LSU had captured its second national championship in school history.

"I just can't tell you how pleased I am that our football team could do something that the state of Louisiana can really, really, really be proud of," Saban said. "And I know they are proud of it. I have never seen such a spirit for an event that I witnessed here in the last couple of days."[13]

The results were not without controversy. USC maintained their number one ranking from the AP as bowl season commenced. When the BCS system snubbed the Trojans, they faced Michigan in the Rose Bowl and had no trouble dispatching the Big Ten champions. When everything on the field had been settled, college football was left with a split national championship. LSU claimed the title from the coaches, and USC was the champ in the eyes of the media. It was the first time since the BCS had been dreamt up by Roy Kramer that a consensus national champion was not crowned. Not that any of it mattered to Saban in the least. The moment the Sugar Bowl ended, he turned his attention to the next season. "You don't really want to know what I'm thinking," Saban replied when asked to describe his emotions. "How are we going to get this accomplished next year? This year's accomplishments are next year's expectations."[14] After the game, Saban approached his quarterback, Matt Mauck. With tape still on his ankles and his head coach walking toward him, Mauck anticipated that congratulations would be forthcoming. "Hey Matt," Saban said. "Are you coming back next year?"[15] Saban never said anything about the game that just ended, having already turned his attention to what was next.

Hyper-focused as he was, Saban would be turning that question back on himself much sooner than anyone at LSU ever anticipated.

* * *

Steve Spurrier coached at Florida five more years after taking the Gators to the top of the college football world in 1996. He captured two more division titles and in 2000 another conference championship, bringing his total SEC titles as coach in Gainesville to six. Following the 2001 season, he resigned as the head coach at Florida. "I simply believe that twelve years as head coach at a major university in the SEC is long enough,"[16] he said, explaining his decision. Ron Zook, a member of Spurrier's staff a decade earlier at Florida but more recently a defensive coordinator in the NFL, was named the new coach. It was a short-lived arrangement. Zook suffered five losses in each of his three seasons as the head coach for Florida. Before the third season ended, it was announced that he would not be returning for a fourth year. Just as LSU had done a few years earlier, the Gators would turn their attention to a young up-and-coming coach who was born and raised in the Midwest.

Urban Meyer was born in Ohio, played high school football in Ohio, and spent his college years as a wide receiver at the University of Cincinnati. After graduation, he spent the majority of the next 15 years at coaching stops all over the Midwest, including five years as the receiver coach at Notre Dame. In 2001, he got his head coaching break at Bowling Green, located in northwestern Ohio. Two successful seasons with the Falcons led Meyer to accept the head job at Utah in 2003, where he quickly turned the above-average program that Ron McBride had established into a powerhouse.

Utah went 10–2 in Meyer's first season in Salt Lake City, including capturing Utah's first outright conference championship since 1957. The Utes began the 2004 season, Meyer's second with the program, ranked twentieth in the nation. A dominating win over Texas A&M in the opening game set Utah on a path to become the very first team from a non–power five conference to earn an invitation to a BCS bowl game. With the Utes wrapping up an unbeaten season, Meyer suddenly became the hottest commodity on the coaching market, and he had Florida and Notre Dame vying for his services.

In early December, parties from both Notre Dame and Florida flew to Salt Lake City on the same day to make their pitch to Meyer, creating a frenzied scene in the usually quiet town. Reporters, fans, and even a news helicopter pursued the Notre Dame contingent as their black limousine made its way from the airport through the downtown streets of Utah's capital city. When Meyer signed his contract with Utah two years earlier, he put language in the deal that allowed him to leave with a relatively small buyout if his destination was one of three schools: Michigan, Ohio State, and Notre Dame. With the Irish in hot pursuit of the young coach, it was believed that South Bend was where he would end up roaming the sidelines. "I'm Irish Catholic, I grew up a Notre Dame fan," Meyer said. "I spent six years there. My son was baptized at Notre Dame. We loved it there."[17] The tradition and mystique of Notre Dame greatly appealed to Meyer, but the opportunity to win big at Florida and the SEC was too great to pass up. He chose the Gators.

Florida signed Meyer to a seven-year, $14 million contract, making him one of the highest-paid college coaches in the country. Years later, Meyer explained his rationale for picking Florida over his dream school. "The bottom line in the coaching profession is you don't have time to build programs anymore. You'd better get it going right now," Meyer said. "Ron Zook was the previous head coach at Florida, I evaluated the rosters the best I could, and I felt Florida had the better roster. Ron Zook [was a] tremendous recruiter. I did my homework and I thought, you know what, you get one swing. And I think the best chance to win is going to be at the University of Florida."[18]

The advice Meyer received from his father matched his own internal instincts. "I told him if you are drawn into the magnitude and aura of Notre Dame and looking at it as some kind of religious crusade then go there and try to win some games," Bud Meyer told his son. "But if you are just going to be a coach, then go to Florida and win a national championship."[19]

Meyer was a pioneer of the spread offense that was beginning to take the nation by storm. He continually innovated and modified his version of the imaginative scheme as the head coach at both Bowling Green and then Utah. Using quarterback Alex Smith, Meyer and the Utes unleashed an offensive attack that few defenses were ready for. Coaches who had faced Meyer's teams warned future SEC foes about what they would be facing. "People are going to catch up with it, just like they catch up with every new innovation on offense, but right now he's got some great ideas where he gives you stretch formations and throwing formations and is able to run option-type plays using the quarterback as an extra running back," New Mexico coach Rocky Long said to a reporter when told that Meyer was off to Florida. "It puts enormous pressure on a defense, and they can outnumber you at times on certain plays and have great success. Right now, he's got the hottest thing going."[20]

Urban Meyer was 40 years old and had never coached in the South. Prior to the press conference to introduce him as the head coach, he had been to Gainesville only one time in his life—on a recruiting trip. He was now tasked with taking over a program that had fired their previous coach even though he never had a losing record at the school. Until Steve Spurrier became the coach at Florida, success had been very limited and sporadic at best in Gainesville. Spurrier was now the standard that every other Gator coach would be held to, as Ron Zook discovered quicker than he ever imagined. Meyer would prove quickly that he could fill the large shoes in the Swamp.

In his first season in Gainesville, Meyer inherited starting quarterback Chris Leak from the previous regime. In 2003, Leak had taken over the duties under center as a freshman and maintained his starting role throughout his sophomore season of 2004. Now an experienced junior, he would be learning his third offensive scheme in as many seasons. Led by Leak, Florida won their first four games in 2005, including a home victory over fifth-ranked Tennessee. But losses against Alabama and LSU knocked the Gators out of the SEC title race. They finished the season strong, closing out Meyer's first year with wins over rival Florida State and against Iowa in the Outback Bowl. With Chris Leak set to come back for another year and Urban Meyer going into his second full off-season of recruiting, the Gators were poised to return to the pedestal that Spurrier had placed them on years earlier.

Much like Nick Saban at LSU, Urban Meyer was a relentless recruiter. Both understood that they would only be as good as the players they surrounded themselves with, and both felt right at home in the SEC. "The Big Ten, or ACC with Miami and Florida State, were always saying they were on par with the SEC, but they weren't any longer when Nick Saban arrived at LSU and when Urban Meyer took over at Florida," said recruiting analyst Tom Lemming. "Those guys did a lot for the SEC in terms of recruiting and getting the SEC to where it is now."[21] Years later, after Meyer had coached at Ohio State following his run at Florida, he compared his experiences. "When I first got to Ohio State, I didn't think the Big Ten was a good recruiting league," he said. "I said that publicly and I got a lot of blowback for that. I didn't [hear about] the other teams like I did in the SEC. In the SEC, you're in a street fight every single day."[22]

Meyer preached to his coaching staff from the very beginning that getting the best players was the only way to build a winner. "I tried to set the bar, as far as phone calls, as far as work, as far as travel, as far as you know, writing letters, emails, text messages," Meyer said. "It was maniacal. It was non-stop."[23] The hard work paid off almost immediately. Ranked first in the nation by ESPN, the 2006 Florida recruiting class that Meyer landed included heralded quarterback Tim Tebow, Percy Harvin (a highly sought-after wide receiver), and linebacker Brandon Spikes. All three would become impact players from the get-go.

The Gators began the 2006 season ranked seventh in the country. Celebrating the 10-year anniversary of their only national championship team as well as honoring the 100th season of football at the university, Florida had their sights set high. After losing three out of the previous four games to Tennessee before Meyer showed up, the Gators beat their rival for the second straight year early in the 2006 season. They followed that up with wins over Alabama and ninth-ranked LSU. Rising to number two in the country, the Gators slipped up the following week against Auburn but rebounded with five consecutive wins. With the streak, Florida had climbed back up to number four in the nation, earning a spot in the SEC Championship Game against eighth-ranked Arkansas. In only his second season, Meyer had the Gators on the precipice of a conference title and, with a little help, something even bigger.

While Florida was trudging through the SEC schedule, Ohio State was flying through their Big Ten slate. The Buckeyes finished their season on November 18 with a perfect 12–0 record and a win in their final game over second-ranked Michigan. With Ohio State firmly established at number one, USC took over the second spot in the polls heading into the final weekend, and Michigan fell one spot to third. The Gators remained fourth.

The 2006 version of the SEC Championship Game was an exciting affair, full of twists and turns, including a result that occurred 3,000 miles away that added to the drama in ways that no one could have predicted. Florida jumped out to a 17–7 lead at halftime, while across the country in Los Angeles, USC was upset by rival UCLA. The Trojans were out of the national title hunt, and Meyer let his team know at halftime that the stakes in the second half had been raised. A win for Florida could allow them to jump Michigan in the polls. In the third quarter, Arkansas fought back and took a 21–17 lead behind star running back Darren McFadden. Fake punts, muffed punts, running backs and wide receivers throwing touchdown passes—it was one for the ages. Late in the game, Percy Harvin erupted for a 67-yard touchdown dash that sealed the win for the Gators, 38–28, and the waiting game began. Had they done enough to jump Michigan in the final polls?

Two years earlier, Auburn went undefeated but was left out of the BCS title game in favor of USC and Oklahoma, both unbeaten as well. The recollection of an SEC team not being chosen was still fresh in the mind of Urban Meyer. As soon as the SEC Championship Game ended, the politicking began.

"I certainly do," Meyer said when asked if he thought that Florida belonged in the national title game. "We deserve a shot. The other team [Michigan] got a shot. I think the country wants to see the SEC champ play the Big Ten." Even in defeat, Arkansas head coach Houston Nutt was pleading the case for the Gators. "I wish more people understand what it is like to go to Auburn, to go to LSU, to go to Tennessee and to try and win in those kinds of places," he said. "What Florida has done is a tremendous accomplishment. They deserve every opportunity that comes their way."[24]

Ohio State head coach Jim Tressel attempted to avoid controversy by withholding his vote from the coaches poll. "I have so much respect for both Michigan and Florida," he said. "Obviously, there are only two teams that had a shot at playing us in the national championship game. I didn't think it was appropriate that Ohio State would cast a ballot one way or the other." But in abstaining from the vote, Tressel irked his Big Ten colleagues, with Michigan coach Lloyd Carr calling it a "slick" move.[25]

When the final BCS tabulations were released the day after the SEC Championship Game, it was Florida that earned the right to face Ohio State, beating Michigan by a hundredth of a point. The Buckeyes were heavily favored going into the game but would quickly wish any other team besides Florida was their opponent. Ohio State started fast, returning the opening kickoff 93 yards for a touchdown. Little else would go right for the Big Ten champs. Florida remained poised and dominated the game the rest of the way, suffocating the prolific Buckeye offense. Heisman-winning quarterback Troy Smith was held to a paltry four completions, and the Ohio State offense managed only 82 yards over the course of the game. The Gator offense had little trouble moving the ball and left no doubt who the best team in the country was with a 41–14 win.

Conference pride remained a talking point in the aftermath, with Florida defensive end Jarvis Moss remarking, "Honestly, we've played a lot better teams than them. I could name four or five teams in the SEC that could probably compete with them and play the same type of game we did against them."[26]

In just two years on the job in Gainesville, Urban Meyer had taken Florida to a place that only Steve Spurrier seemed to know the directions to previously. The Gators were kings of the college football world, as was the SEC once again. The conference had their first national championship since Nick Saban and LSU won the title three years earlier. With many key players returning, it was assumed that Meyer was at the beginning of a Gator dynasty. And while Florida was in fact primed for a dominating run, the 2006 national championship for the Gators represented a much larger development. It was the inception of the most incredible stretch of college football success any conference had ever known.

CHAPTER 9

The Reign Begins

THE 2006 FLORIDA GATOR NATIONAL CHAMPIONSHIP TEAM WAS A combination of veteran players recruited by previous head coach Ron Zook and younger players brought to the program by Urban Meyer. Heading into the 2007 season, many of the impact players were gone, including losing nine of 11 starters on defense. Much of the attention was focused on quarterback, where Tim Tebow was being handed the reins.

As a freshman, Tebow was the backup quarterback during the 2006 season and saw playing time as a change of pace to starter Chris Leak. Inserted into the game mostly as a running threat, Tebow rushed for eight touchdowns in his first season of college football. He also threw five touchdown passes, including the famous "jump pass" against LSU to help seal the victory. But the former high school all-American almost ended up at a rival SEC school rather than in Gainesville.

Tebow was born in the Philippines to parents who had moved there years earlier to establish a ministry as Baptist missionaries. When he was three years old, the family moved back to the United States and settled in Jacksonville, Florida. Tebow was homeschooled, but Florida laws allowed him to compete on the local high school football team. His career at Nease High School became legendary. During his junior season, he suffered a leg injury in the first half of a game late in the season. Believing that it was cramps, he played the remainder of the game and ran for a 29-yard touchdown. Only after the game was over was it discovered that he had a broken fibula. His work ethic and competitiveness drove him to work harder than anyone around him, and he was rewarded by being named the Florida High School Player of the Year after both his junior and senior seasons. Because he was so highly recruited, making the decision on where to play college football wasn't an easy decision.

Tebow ultimately narrowed his options down to two SEC schools: Florida, where his parents met and enjoyed their first date at a Florida–Georgia football game, and Alabama, where he had built a strong connection with Tide head coach Mike Shula. Leading up to Tebow's decision and understanding the impact he would make on a program, Urban Meyer was getting nervous. "I remember, already in my mind, convincing myself that we lost Tim," he said. "And there was a junior college quarterback we were set to go see because in my mind, we lost Tim to Alabama. I'm getting on the plane with [assistant coach] Greg Mattison . . . I looked at him and said 'We're going to be okay. I have a plan in case Tim goes to Alabama.'"

"I started explaining this plan and Greg puts his hand up, and said 'Coach, if we lose Tim Tebow to Alabama, that will set the program back 10 years.' I got so upset because I knew he was right."[1]

Meyer's instincts weren't that far off. Tebow was struggling to make a decision. He went through the exercise of building a pros-and-cons list and discussing it with his parents. In a moment of desperation, he pleaded with his dad to tell him where to go. His father replied by asking him that if it all came down to making the choice based on just one person, who it would be. Tebow knew at that moment that he would be going to Florida because of his belief in Urban Meyer, and he set out to inform both Meyer and Shula of his decision. His first call was to the Alabama coach.

"The right thing was to call coach Shula and tell him I'm not going to Alabama," Tebow said. "I started crying when I was talking to him. I'm talking to him and I said, 'Hey, Coach Shula, I'm so sorry. I'm not going to go to Alabama. I'm going to Florida.' He says, 'Timmy, you stop right there. I love you just as much now as if you came to Alabama. You're going to have a great career and hopefully I'll coach you one day.'"

"So, I hang up the phone and I look at my dad and say, 'That's the coach I'm supposed to play for. I just told him I'm going to Florida and he says he loves me!'"[2]

Even though Tebow was moved by the reaction of Mike Shula, he regained his composure enough to stick with his decision of attending Florida. He immediately picked up the phone to call Urban Meyer and let him know the good news, but his emotions were still very much present and audible from his call with Shula.

"I'm driving home and my cell phone rings and it's Tim," Meyer recalled. "I'm like, 'Oh, man, here we go.' He's like, 'Hey coach' and he's crying. He said, 'I've made a decision to go' . . . and the phone goes out."[3]

The call dropped. Tebow was frantically trying to get Meyer back on the phone, but it would not connect. Meyer tried dialing Tebow back but had no success. Heightening the drama, this was all taking place moments before Tebow was set to appear on television to announce where he would be playing. Having arrived home and convinced that Tebow was trying to alert him of bad news, Meyer couldn't stand to watch and went into the yard.

After being shoved out onstage at his high school and without finishing his conversation with Meyer, the college choice was revealed: Tebow would be a Florida Gator just like his parents. Meyer's wife and children remained in the house and began hollering. Meyer got his guy after all.

After spot duty as a freshman, Tim Tebow was ready to assume the reins of the defending national champions heading into the 2007 season. "You get asked how you deal with the pressure [of playing quarterback for Florida]," he said. "You think about it like football isn't the most important thing in the world. There are things more important every day. Going to the Philippines with my dad [who was a missionary there] and being in the orphanage and thinking if you could get your whole life wrapped up in what is going to happen on fourth down instead of thinking it is a blessing to play football. That takes a lot of pressure off."[4]

The defending national champions jumped out to a 4–0 start but lost back-to-back games to Auburn and LSU. Two weeks later, a loss to Georgia for only the third time in 10 years dropped the Gators to 5–3 on the year and out of contention for the SEC title. The season wasn't living up to the high standards that had been set in Gainesville for the program, but for Tebow personally, he was enjoying a breakout year. The Gators finished the regular season with four consecutive wins, and Tebow shattered records along the way. He ended the year with 20 rushing touchdowns and 55 combined touchdowns, both single-season records in the SEC. The year was capped off with Tebow becoming the first sophomore to win the Heisman, joining Steve Spurrier and Danny Wuerffel as Florida quarterbacks to win the award. It was the first Heisman for an SEC school since Wuerffel won 10 years earlier and only the fourth in the previous 35 years.

While Tebow was busy running over everything and everyone in front of him in 2007, LSU was busy getting back to the heights that Nick Saban had taken them to only a few years earlier. Following the 2005 season, Saban bolted the SEC for the NFL, accepting an offer to become head coach of the Miami Dolphins. "Everybody is presented with difficult decisions in their life, career decisions that affect a lot of people in their life, and this was certainly one," Saban said at the time. "We weren't seeking [this] opportunity. It's never a good time to do these things when you're happy. I just felt like this opportunity with this organization was one of the best that's ever been offered to me." It wouldn't be long before another opportunity came his way that would be too promising to pass up.[5]

Les Miles was brought in from Oklahoma State to replace Saban and keep the LSU program humming along. By his third season at the helm, he had the Tigers playing in the BCS Championship Game albeit through unusual circumstances. LSU lost two games in the regular season, both in triple overtime and both as the top-ranked team in the country. A wild final weekend of college football featuring multiple upsets vaulted the Tigers back into the picture, and they faced Ohio State for the title. Just like four years earlier, the game was played in New Orleans and acted as a de facto home game for the Tigers. However, the outcome was never in doubt. LSU controlled the game from the start and led, 24–10, at halftime. Cruising in the second half to a 38–24 victory, the Tigers won the national championship and in the process became the first school to have multiple BCS titles to their credit. It was also the second consecutive national championship for the SEC, the first time the conference had accomplished that feat since Alabama and Georgia combined to win three straight in 1978–1980. Urban Meyer was going to make sure that the SEC streak continued.

With Tim Tebow returning at quarterback, along with all-Americans Percy Harvin and Brandon Spikes, the Gators opened the 2008 season ranked fifth in the nation. After easily winning their first three games, including a 30–6 beatdown of rival Tennessee, the Gators inexplicably lost at home to unranked Ole Miss. It was a devastating defeat for a team that was expected to contend for the national championship.

Following the game, Tebow gave an emotional speech to conclude his remarks to the media. "I just wanted to say one thing to Gator Nation," he said, taking a deep sigh and choking back tears before continuing. "I'm sorry. I'm extremely sorry. We were hoping for an undefeated season. That was my goal, something Florida's never done here, but I promise you one thing, a lot of good will come out of this. You have never seen any player in the entire country play as hard as I will play the rest of this season and you'll never see someone push the rest of the team as hard as I will push everybody the rest of this season and you'll never see a team play harder than we will the rest of this season. God bless."[6] The remarks became known in Gator lore as "The Promise," and it propelled Florida to a victory in every game the remainder of the season.

The inspired Gators rolled through the rest of their schedule, winning their final eight regular season games by a combined 317 points, including beating top-ranked Alabama in the SEC Championship Game. In the BCS Championship Game in South Florida, the Gators capped off Tebow's promise by defeating Oklahoma, 24–14, to capture the national title. It was the second championship in three years for the Florida football program and the third consecutive title for the SEC.

As a senior, Tebow broke a revered SEC record set by Herschel Walker nearly 30 years earlier, rushing for 55 career touchdowns. He had become one of the most popular and transcendent players in college football history. After being taken in the first round of the NFL draft by the Denver Broncos, his jersey became the fastest-selling rookie jersey in league history. His NFL popularity score was second behind another

SEC legend: Peyton Manning. "I've never seen an athlete command a field as [Tim Tebow] did," Urban Meyer said. "The number one trait of a quarterback is a competitor. And he's the most competitive person I've ever met in my life."[7] Tebow departed Florida with two national titles, a Heisman Trophy, and dozens of school records. Urban Meyer would leave Florida under less desirable circumstances.

"After we won the national title in 2008, we were in there celebrating and I went in and closed the door to my locker room so I could email and text recruits," Meyer confessed years later. "One of the other coaches came in and said, 'What the hell are you doing?' I was already on to the next one. I never really sat back."[8]

The internal pressure Meyer put on himself eventually led to his taking a leave of absence following the 2009 season due to health concerns. He rejoined the team in March 2010, but it would be his final year as the head coach of the Florida Gators, as he stepped down from the position at the conclusion of the season. Even with the unceremonious exit, Meyer had changed the SEC forever.

* * *

As the SEC began a run of national championships with the 2006 Florida Gators, college football fans all over the country began to take a much greater interest in the conference. Several factors—including the emergence of the BCS a decade earlier, the continued impact that the SEC Championship Game had on which schools were selected for the BCS, and the SEC on CBS game of the week throughout the season—led to the historically regional conference gaining a powerful national following. Television viewership for the conference had begun a steady climb throughout the early 2000s, increasing year after year as the contract term with the networks was coming to an end.

Over the course of the 2006 season, the SEC on CBS was the only college football property on TV to see an increase from the previous year. Even though the ratings were slightly lower than ABC's regional coverage of other conferences, the conference was gaining momentum. In 2007, CBS gained another 13 percent in viewership of SEC games and posted their most watched season since 1999. It presented perfect timing for the conference as they began negotiations with the networks for their next TV contract. What they came away with was a staggering amount of money that the conference leaders fighting decades earlier in the Supreme Court could never have imagined.

In 2006, the Big Ten signed a $1 billion, 10-year contract with ESPN and ABC. Only two years later, the SEC would reset the market and established their conference as the preeminent TV property in college football.

In early August 2008, SEC commissioner Mike Slive announced a new 15-year contract with CBS for a reported $55 million per season. "The SEC is the gold standard in college athletics," said Mike Aresco, CBS's executive vice president for sports programming. "The length of this deal is a testament to the great brand that The SEC on CBS has become."[9]

Two weeks later, Slive made another announcement, this time high-lighting the SEC's new contract with ESPN. Just like CBS, the cable giant had also agreed to a 15-year deal but for considerably more money. ESPN would be paying the SEC $2.25 billion over the length of the contract. "We're thrilled with the historic nature of this deal," ESPN executive vice president John Skipper said, adding that college sports have been "part of our DNA" for nearly 30 years. "It's not hard to figure why we'd want to be involved with it, given the quality of SEC sports, for 15 more years."[10]

Mike Slive revealed that he had been involved in negotiations for nearly two years. He was exhausted but had delivered a financial package that would allow the SEC and its schools to continue to dominate on the gridiron. "The bottom line here is that fans of SEC football will have more access to games and better distribution than they ever have in the past," he said. "In the truest sense of the word we got our cake and ate it too. I'm ready to go watch some football."[11]

The individual members of the SEC were beyond elated. "It's huge. There's nothing like it in the history of college athletics," South Carolina athletic director Eric Hyman said. "In the history of the Southeastern Conference this might be one of the defining moments."[12]

The 2009 season rewarded the networks that partnered with the SEC immediately as the momentum both on and off the field continued to build. CBS and ESPN ended the year with their best ratings in more than a decade. CBS in particular reached a milestone. They averaged seven million viewers over the 15-game SEC broadcast schedule, which was more than a million higher than the 2008 season. But more important, they bested their rival network in the ratings, as ABC averaged 6.1 million viewers over the course of the 2009 college football season. It took a decade, but CBS's gamble of putting a southern conference on national television week after week had paid off.

"The SEC on CBS has become the premier package in college football. With just one national game a week, the SEC on CBS has been the highest-rated college football package," said Mike Aresco. "CBS is privileged to televise these great teams and athletes each week and to capture the pageantry and drama of the conference."[13]

Eighteen million viewers tuned in to watch the 2009 SEC Championship Game, illustrating how far the conference had traveled over the years, from being pushed aside by the television networks in the 1950s to showcase schools from the North to having to fight with the NCAA to gain the ability to negotiate TV contracts as a conference. It was the most watched regular season college football game in the country that year and the highest rated non-bowl game in four years. The number of viewers nearly doubled from two years prior. Armed with new TV deals that paid the conference billions of dollars and on a three-year streak of winning the national title, the SEC was poised for a dominating run that had never taken place previously for any conference, with Nick Saban leading the way.

* * *

After winning the national championship in 1992 under coach Gene Stallings, the Alabama Crimson Tide had a difficult time reaching the pinnacle of the sport again. They competed in three of the next four conference title games but lost all of them to Steve Spurrier and his Florida Gators. Stallings retired following the 1996 season, setting in motion a

10-year stretch of poor coaching hires, seasons marred by NCAA probation, and mostly forgettable football by Alabama standards.

Mike DuBose, a former player for Bear Bryant in the 1970s, was hired to replace Stallings. He began his tenure by presiding over the first losing season in Tuscaloosa since 1984, and he never truly recovered. Months before his third season at the helm, a sexual harassment complaint was filed by his secretary, with whom he was having an affair. He admitted to the wrongdoing, settled out of court, and had two years removed from his contract with the university. He followed the scandal by guiding Alabama to the conference championship in what would be their only such title between 1993 and 2008. However, the following season, everything fell apart for DuBose. The team finished 3–8, the fewest wins at Alabama since 1957, and DuBose was fired midyear.

Dennis Franchione was hired after a successful run at TCU, but his stay in Tuscaloosa lasted only two years. Frustrated by NCAA sanctions, he bolted for Texas A&M following a 10–3 mark in his second season. In December 2002, Alabama turned to Washington State coach Mike Price to lead the program, but the gregarious coach never walked the sidelines for the Tide. He was fired five months later after a wild night at a topless bar and a $1,000 room service charge on his hotel bill. With the program in turmoil and on probation, Alabama turned to former star quarterback Mike Shula prior to the 2003 season. With the SEC being dominated by Nick Saban at LSU, followed by Urban Meyer at Florida, Shula was unable to bring his alma mater back to the top. Following a fifth straight Alabama loss in the Iron Bowl to Auburn, Shula was fired in November 2006.

In the nearly 25 years following the retirement of Bear Bryant in 1982, Alabama had employed seven different coaches and had only three SEC championships and one national title to show for it. The once-proud program that years earlier had been the very essence of championship football in the SEC was desperate to find a coach who could re-create the mystique, the religion even, that Bryant had built. They would find their deliverer in a coach who was adrift in the turbulent seas of the NFL.

In December 2004, after coaching LSU for five seasons and winning a national championship, Nick Saban left Baton Rouge for the Miami

Dolphins and the NFL. His foray into professional football didn't last long. Even though he had five years' experience as an assistant in the NFL earlier in his career, he did not enjoy the success he was accustomed to as a head coach. His first season in Miami was off to a promising start, as the Dolphins finished 9–7 and just missed out on the playoffs. In the offseason, Saban and the team pursued free agent quarterback Drew Brees, eventually signing him to a contract. But Brees failed the physical because of a shoulder injury, and the Dolphins refused to go through with the deal. Brees ended up in New Orleans, and the Dolphins sputtered to a 6–10 record in 2006, the first losing season for Nick Saban as a head coach.

Lacking the control over player personnel that he was accustomed to in college, Saban knew that his days in the NFL were numbered. "I decided right then when [the Dolphins didn't sign Brees] that we don't have a quarterback in the NFL, we're not going to win. I'm getting out of here. I'm not staying here. I'm not going to be responsible for this."[14]

Alabama athletic director Mal Moore knew that the pressure was on. The previous athletic director had been fired because of the Mike DuBose coaching fiasco. Moore had to get this hire right. He contacted Nick Saban's agent in November and was told that Saban would not leave the Dolphins until the season was over. His next call was to Steve Spurrier, who the year before came back to the SEC. "Moore called me and I had just taken the job at South Carolina," Spurrier said. "I had just been there one year and I told him, 'Nah, I'm committed to these guys, this is where I'm going to finish up.'"[15] Moore's first two choices had turned him down.

With recruiting in full swing, the situation was getting more precarious every day that passed without a coach. Moore targeted West Virginia head coach Rich Rodriguez, at the time one of the hottest offensive minds in college football. Hours before the awards dinner for the National Football Foundation in New York City in early December, Moore interviewed Rodriguez. The discussion went well, and both sides came away with the understanding that they would be making a formal announcement after details were ironed out. "Rodriguez was very, very interested in the position and basically gave a verbal acceptance of it," said Chuck Neinas, whom Moore had retained as his search consultant. Word of the impending hire soon leaked to the media, and the *Birmingham News* published a story with the details that Rich Rodriguez would be coming to Alabama. Two short days later, everything changed. Given the opportunity to attempt to keep Rodriguez, West Virginia put forward an attractive raise and a commitment to improve the athletic facilities. It was enough to keep the former Mountaineer player in Morgantown. Rodriguez announced that he was staying at West Virginia.

The news stunned Mal Moore, and he was compelled to issue a statement. "I received word this afternoon that Coach Rodriguez has chosen to remain the head football coach at West Virginia," Moore said. "I fully respect his decision and wish him the best. I want to remind everyone of what I said at the outset of this process: my only objective is to get the best person available to lead the Alabama football program."[16] It was a development that would alter the history of not only Alabama and the SEC but also college football in general. After getting snubbed by Rodriguez, Moore turned his attention back to the coach he wanted from the beginning: Nick Saban.

When the news broke out of Tuscaloosa that Mike Shula had been fired, Nick Saban was forced to go on the defensive immediately. "I had a good college job so why would I have left that if I was going to be interested in other college jobs," Saban curtly told the media the day after Shula was let go. "I took [the Dolphins job] as a challenge and we certainly haven't seen this through and gotten where we wanted to go and finished the job here, so why would I be interested in something else?"[17]

By mid-December, with the Alabama job still open, the rumors surrounding Saban had reached a fever pitch, and the prickly coach blurted out a declaration that he would later regret. "I guess I have to say it. I'm not going to be the coach at Alabama. I'm telling you there's no significance about this, about any interest that I have in anything other than being the coach here in Miami."[18]

While the drama was playing out publicly and the heat from Alabama fans was intensifying, Mal Moore was quietly yet persistently working the back channels to get his man. He had been in contact with Saban's agent, Jimmy Sexton, and had received assurances that Saban would be interested in the Alabama job. But Saban remained steadfast in his position of not personally meeting with Moore until the Dolphins concluded their season. Without a meeting scheduled with Saban, Moore flew to Miami on New Year's Day to be in town after the Dolphins played their final game of the year. When Sexton asked Moore what he would do if the gamble didn't pay off and Saban declined to join him at Alabama, Moore replied, "I'm not going back to Alabama. I think I'll just have them take me down to Cuba."[19]

Moore checked into his hotel and began calling Saban but was unsuccessful after multiple attempts. Finally, late into the evening, Saban called back. Along with his wife Terry, Saban spoke with Moore for an hour, listening to the Alabama athletic director explain why he was the perfect fit for the job. The conversation ended with Saban telling Moore that he would call the following day. After standing by the phone all day for a call that never came, Moore headed back to the airport disheartened. Just before departing, he got a call from Sexton telling him to wait one more day. With more than a dozen coaches contacting Alabama to express interest in the job, the clock was ticking. But Moore agreed and hunkered down in South Florida for another night.

After again waiting most of the day for any word from Saban or Sexton, Moore grew impatient. In a final attempt to close the deal, he drove to the Saban house unannounced and knocked on the door. Terry Saban answered and invited him in. With Nick away at the Dolphins facility meeting with ownership, Moore turned on the charm with Terry, painting a picture for what her family life would be like in Tuscaloosa and why her husband was perfect for the job.

After a long day of meetings with the Dolphins, Nick called his wife to let her know that he was on his way home. "I don't think I'm even going to be able talk to Moore tonight," he said.

"Oh, Mal's already here," Terry replied to her husband. "We've been talking for over an hour." It turned out to be the most important hour that Mal Moore had spent the entire coaching search. With Terry already convinced that leaving Miami for Tuscaloosa was the right move, Moore went to work on Nick and before long had him persuaded to make the leap. Nick Saban would be the next head football coach at Alabama.[20]

Saban and Alabama agreed on an eight-year, $32 million contract. He became the highest-paid coach in college football and would be making more money than most coaches in the NFL. At the press conference, University of Alabama president Robert E. Witt was sure that they had the right man for the job. "We are confident that coach Saban's proven record as a head coach and his commitment to the success of our student athletes, on and off the field, combined with the best facilities in America and the passion of tens of thousands of Crimson Tide fans across the nation will lead to many years of success at the championship level."[21] He would have no idea how right that statement would prove to be.

Showing that he understood exactly what he was getting into, Saban met the challenge in front of him head-on. "I know there's tremendous expectations here for what you would like to accomplish with this football program," he said to the fans at the press conference. "I can tell you that however you feel about it, I have even higher expectations for what we want to accomplish. I want to win every game we play."[22]

As soon as Saban took over in Tuscaloosa, he hit the recruiting trail. Alabama had failed to land a top 10 recruiting class the previous five seasons. In 2007, Saban brought the Crimson Tide back into the top echelon of the rankings. It was a bumpy first season for Saban, as Alabama finished 7–6 in 2007 with a win over Colorado in the Independence Bowl. In 2008, the Tide began the season ranked twenty-fourth, but after pummeling ninth-ranked Clemson in the opener, they jumped 11 spots and put everyone on notice. They followed with 11 wins in a row, including beating Auburn, 36–0, handing the Tigers their worst loss in the Iron Bowl since 1962. Alabama was the top-ranked team in the nation heading into the SEC Championship Game, where they met Tim Tebow and the Florida Gators. Not able to keep up with the future national champions, Alabama lost the game, sending them to New Orleans for their first Sugar Bowl appearance since clinching the national title there following the 1992 season. An inspired Utah team walloped the Crimson Tide in the game, but the truth remained: in two short years, Nick Saban had turned around Alabama, and a sleeping giant was ready to reclaim its spot among the elite in college football.

With 16 returning starters, Alabama began the 2009 season as the fifth-ranked team in the country. They opened the year by facing seventh-ranked Virginia Tech in a neutral site clash at the Georgia Dome, where they hoped to return in December and claim their first SEC title since 1999. A 34–22 win over the Hokies set Nick Saban's squad on their way. With wins over ranked SEC foes Ole Miss, South Carolina, and LSU scattered throughout the season, the Crimson Tide won every game they played on their way back to Atlanta. Waiting for Saban and Alabama were the top-ranked Florida Gators, led by quarterback Tim Tebow. Urban Meyer's team was also unbeaten, setting up a showdown for the ages, exactly the type of scenario that Roy Kramer had dreamt about nearly 20 years earlier when the SEC Championship Game was created. It would be the first time a championship game in any conference featured two undefeated teams. If a phone call had been returned 20 years earlier, it might not have taken place at all.

In 1990, Toledo hired 39-year-old Nick Saban, giving the ambitious defensive mind his first head coaching job. Twenty-five-year-old Urban Meyer was making $10,000 per year coaching quarterbacks and receivers at Illinois State when he called the Saban house, hoping to get a job on the Toledo staff and come home to Ohio. But rather than reaching Nick, his wife Terry answered the phone. "We chatted for about 10 minutes," Meyer remembered. "I got her. She was sold on me. She was ready to go. I remember telling my fiancée, 'Looks like we're going back to Ohio.'" Terry promised to have Nick reach out to Urban, but the call never came. "I didn't know [Meyer] from Adam's house cat," Saban explained. Urban took a job at Colorado State, and the two would never work on the same staff together.[23]

Standing across the field from Urban Meyer in the 2009 SEC Championship Game, Nick Saban was in a good mood early. Alabama jumped out to a 9–0 lead in the first quarter and never looked back on their way to a dominating 32–13 win over the Gators. While the on-field drama didn't live up to the hype, the SEC still capitalized. With 17.9 million viewers, it was the most watched college football game of the 2009 season on any network and was the highest-rated SEC Championship Game of all time. "The SEC has the best conference in college football and a fanbase that surrounds it that any marketer would dream to have," said Paul Swangard, managing director of the Warsaw Sports Marketing Center at the University of Oregon.[24] One month after winning the conference championship, Alabama would cement the SEC's dominance in the college football landscape.

Returning to the exact location where nearly 100 years later earlier Alabama first staked their claim as the superior college football program in the country, the Crimson Tide faced Texas in the BCS Championship Game at the Rose Bowl in Pasadena. The outcome was never truly in doubt. Alabama scored 24 unanswered points in the second quarter to take a commanding lead and finished off the Longhorns with a 37–21 win. At long last, the very best team in college football again resided in Tuscaloosa.

With the win, Alabama claimed their first national title since 1992. It was the fourth in a row for the SEC and the fifth in seven years. No conference had won four consecutive AP national titles until this run by the SEC. Incredibly, this wasn't the end for the conference; it was still in the early stages of taking over college football.

CHAPTER 10

"SEC, SEC, SEC!"

As THE SEC MOVED INTO THE 2010S, THEY FOUND THEMSELVES ON top of the college football universe, a destination no one could have imagined when the conference formed nearly 80 years earlier. It had been a long road from their humble and controversial beginning when they split from the Southern Conference in December 1932. Bob Murphy, columnist for the *Knoxville Journal*, wrote at the time, "A great day is ahead for the ten members, who remained in the Southern Conference and who now can enjoy their athletics in peace—without fear of having their heads chopped off with one fell swoop of a political monarch."[1] Even though Murphy incorrectly assumed that the Southern Conference would end up as the stronger conference after the split, his comments were otherwise insightful. While the SEC enjoys a healthy competitiveness within conference games, conference pride takes precedence when lining up against another conference. "SEC! SEC! SEC!" The chant echoes from fans when facing a school from outside the conference.

With the SEC looking to make it five national titles in a row, the 2010 season opened with defending champion Alabama as the number one team in the nation. A back-to-back championship run would have to wait for the Tide, as their Iron Bowl rivals stole the show. Starting the year ranked twenty-third, the Tigers won game after game, eventually meeting Alabama at the end of the season as the second-ranked team in the country. The SEC again had the highest-rated game of the season on TV, as the nation watched Auburn beat Alabama, 28–27. The following week, the Tigers pummeled South Carolina, 56–17, to earn a shot at their first national title since Shug Jordan coached the 1957 squad. Behind Heisman-winning quarterback Cam Newton, Auburn beat Oregon in the BCS National Championship in early January. The SEC had now won five consecutive national championships.

The 2011 college football season would prove to be the year when the consistent high level of play in the SEC would help the conference do something that had never been done before. Alabama began the season ranked second in the country, while conference rival LSU was fourth. By the time the schools met in early November, the Tigers had jumped to number one, and Alabama remained at number two. In the first-ever regular season matchup between SEC schools ranked one and two, LSU came out on top, with a 9–6 overtime win.

LSU continued to win running the table the remainder of the regular season, claiming the SEC championship and a spot in the BCS title game in New Orleans. Alabama fell only one spot after the loss to the Tigers. Now ranked third in the country, they waited for help, which came in the form of a cyclone. Second-ranked Oklahoma State was upset in double overtime by Iowa State on November 18. The defeat dropped the Cowboys to third and moved Alabama up to second. Much to the dismay of many around the country, the BCS National Championship Game would feature two teams from the SEC, including one, Alabama, that didn't even win its own division. Nick Saban apologized to no one.

"Oklahoma State has a really, really good football team," Saban said after the announcement. "But rather than rehash the system, the system that we have worked the way it did. The two teams that came out on top are in the game. I'm sure that if we were in their position, we would be a little disappointed about that, and I understand that. But it's the system that we have and rather than rehash the system, I think maybe we should do research on what would make the system better in the future."[2] With Alabama facing LSU for the BCS title in 2011, the conference was guaranteed a sixth straight national champion.

Even though the SEC came under fire for supplying both teams to the BCS, 24 million people tuned in to watch Alabama shut out LSU, 21–0, to win the 2011 college football national championship. It was Nick Saban's third title as head coach and second at Alabama. The Tide would follow that up with another national championship in 2012. Alabama beat historical rival Notre Dame, 42–14, to give the program back-to-back national titles. It was the first time since Bear Bryant led the Tide to consecutive titles in 1978–1979 that Alabama had accomplished the feat. For the SEC, their eminence continued to grow.

Following the game, *Sports Illustrated* college football writer Michael Rosenberg summed it up. "Football is the South's thing, and the SEC's thing, and you might be sick of it, but that doesn't change the truth. The rest of the country is playing catch-up, and not playing it particularly well. Just admit it, everybody. Alabama was the best team in the nation this year, and it wasn't close. The SEC is better, and it isn't close. At this point, the rest of the country's best hope for a national title is secession."[3]

Alabama's win over Notre Dame in the BCS title game marked the seventh consecutive national championship for the SEC. While the conference was continuing its steady presence at the top of the rankings, change occurred in its membership for the first time since Roy Kramer invited Arkansas and South Carolina 20 years earlier.

Texas A&M considered joining the SEC in the past, but each time, Lone Star State politicians had gotten involved and squashed any ideas that the folks in College Station had of heading east. In 2011, under the leadership of school president R. Bowen Loftin, the Aggies were finally able to get out from under the shadow of the rival Texas Longhorns. They had television to thank for it.

Two years earlier, attending his first Big 12 meeting as the president of Texas A&M, Loftin saw firsthand the power that Texas wielded. "That was sort of eye-opening," he said. "It was pretty clear how things worked. One school was pretty much in charge of how the conference was going to go. [Big 12 commissioner Dan] Beebe was clearly beholden to that school. That gave me pause." In 2010, the Aggies came close to making a move when Colorado bolted the Big 12 for the Pac-12 and Nebraska left for greener pastures of the Big Ten. Hanging by a thread, the Big 12 stuck together. The peace lasted only a year, and everything changed in 2011, when Texas and ESPN announced a 20-year deal that would pay the school $300 million and create the Longhorn Network. It was the last straw for Loftin.[4]

"When the Longhorn Network was announced, that just galvanized our former and current students," Loftin said, saying that there were suddenly fewer people on the fence about breaking ranks and leaving the conference and splitting with the Longhorns. "We went from 50–50 to 95–5 [in favor of the SEC] almost overnight."[5]

Finally free from political pressures to remain in the same conference with Texas, the Aggies pursued membership in the SEC. Anxious to add the Lone Star State to its ranks, the SEC expanded, announcing the addition of Texas A&M on September 25, 2011. Less than two months later, the conference expanded again as they added the University of Missouri, picking up the Kansas City and St. Louis television markets. Beginning with the 2012 season, the SEC would be 14 members strong.

At the conclusion of the 2013 season, the SEC again found itself with a representative in the BCS National Championship Game, with the Auburn Tigers looking to continue the remarkable streak of winning it all. Up on Florida State, 21–3, it seemed all but certain that the SEC would end up on top again. But it was not to be. The Seminoles stormed back, ultimately defeating Auburn, 34–31, by scoring the go-ahead touchdown with only 13 seconds left. After an impossible seven straight national championships, the SEC had finally been dethroned. In 2014, the first year of the College Football Playoff, the SEC would come up short again, as the Urban Meyer–led Ohio State Buckeyes would capture the crown. Order was restored in the 2015 season, with Alabama winning another national championship, their fourth under Saban. Clemson burst onto the scene the following year and won both the 2016 and the 2018 national titles. But other than those two seasons, it has been all SEC in recent memory. The Crimson Tide brought home the prize in 2017 and 2020, with Saban using the latter championship to tie Bear Bryant with six national titles in Tuscaloosa. LSU, led by prolific passer Joe Burrow, won it all in 2019, and that was followed by back-to-back national championships captured by Georgia, with former Saban assistant Kirby Smart patrolling the sidelines in Athens.

With national championships happening year after year and TV viewership hitting all-time highs, the SEC was turning into an unstoppable force. Nowhere did that become more apparent than in recruiting.

When Nick Saban and Alabama athletic director Mal Moore were flying from Miami to Tuscaloosa to introduce Saban as the new head coach, Saban turned to Moore and said, "Mal, you must think I'm a helluva good coach. There are a lot of good coaches out there, but I know how to recruit and get difference makers. I can't coach without great players." Moore, a former quarterback for Bear Bryant, knew more than anyone the heart of college football was recruiting. "Nick, that's the best thing I've heard you say," came the reply from Moore.[6] Nick Saban not only turned Alabama into the number one destination for high school recruits but also led the way for his SEC contemporaries.

In the five years before Saban took over at Alabama, the Crimson Tide did not finish ranked in the top 10 recruiting classes nationally on Rivals.com, a website that evaluates college football recruiting. From 2007 through 2023, Alabama was in the top 10 every year, many times finishing with the top-ranked class in the country. Beginning with the 2013 recruiting class, the SEC had at least five programs ranked in the top 10 nationally every year through 2021 with one exception. In two of those years, 2014 and 2020, the SEC claimed an incredible seven of the top 10 spots.

The pressure to win and to recruit the players who will allow a school to win in the SEC is fueled in part by the financial windfall that conference members have received over the years. In 2019, Georgia spent a staggering $3.6 million on recruiting. In the same year, Alabama spent $2.6 million, while other schools, such as South Carolina, spent $931,000. Georgia and Alabama ended the recruiting cycle in 2019 with the top-ranked classes in the country.

Kirby Smart knows it takes a small army to win in recruiting. "The academic people at the University of Georgia who sacrificed their Saturdays, their Sundays and their countless hours. I don't think people really understand that recruiting never sleeps," he said. "But this [recruiting class] goes back to the sacrifices that everybody gave to give their time and make the effort. We've got kids coming from Texas, from California, and all over the country. People have to give their time for us to have the opportunity to sign players like this."[7]

With more and more of the best high school players choosing to play for SEC schools and the interest of fans continuing to grow, a conference-centric television network was the next natural step. Rival conferences like the Big Ten and Pac-12 had created their own networks years earlier, but ESPN had made it worthwhile financially for the SEC to refrain. That all changed in May 2013, when ESPN and the SEC announced the creation of the SEC Network, with the partners signing a 20-year agreement and looking to continue to broaden the reach of the SEC brand.

"The SEC Network is not a regional network. This is a national network," ESPN president John Skipper said. "We understand that within the 11-state footprint is where the most passionate fan base is, the most important fan base, but there's a lot of SEC fans in California, Michigan, Connecticut, Nebraska."[8]

In addition to creating their own network, the SEC was beginning to look ahead to when their contract with CBS would expire after the 2023 season. When the conference expanded by adding Texas A&M and Missouri, they looked to renegotiate with their current broadcast partners. ESPN was willing, but CBS was not. The 15-year deal CBS had signed with the SEC in 2008 came only a couple years before an explosion of value in sports rights on TV, and it turned into the deal of the century for CBS. In December 2020, the SEC announced a new 10-year, $3 billion agreement with ESPN. Beginning with the 2024 season, every SEC sporting event would be broadcast on the ESPN family of networks.

"This is a significant day for the Southeastern Conference and for the future of our member institutions," said SEC commissioner Greg Sankey. "Our agreement with ESPN will greatly enhance our ability to support our student-athletes in the years ahead and to further enrich the game day experience for SEC fans around the world.

"The broadcast industry's intense and widespread interest in securing the SEC's first tier rights is a direct reflection of the sustained excellence achieved by our 14 member schools, and we are thrilled to have been able to maximize our current position of strength to benefit our student-athletes, the fans who go to our games, and home viewers."[9]

With CBS losing the rights to SEC football, fans immediately wanted to know what would happen to the theme music that they had grown so fond of hearing over the years on Saturday afternoon. "I think [the music] has come up in every interview," ESPN executive vice president Burke Magnus said, hoping to reassure the fans. "I have tremendous respect for CBS. The coverage they've provided the conference for so many years has been outstanding. That theme music is part of it. I'm as big a college football fan as anybody. I enjoy it the same way other fans do. It's iconic. I'm quite confident we'll come up with a really awesome, innovative presentation of the highest caliber and the highest quality for the SEC on our networks."[10]

The number of fans watching at home continued to grow year after year as the SEC built itself into a national brand. Four million viewers for a college football broadcast is seen inside the television industry as the amount needed to continue to drive exorbitant fees from the networks. From 2015 through the 2022 season, Alabama led the nation with 50 games that exceeded 4 million viewers. Six of the top 10 spots were occupied by SEC schools, a staggering number when considering that only three states with an SEC presence are in the top 15 highest-populated states in the country.

Heading into the 2020s, the SEC seemed perfectly positioned for continued dominance. Off the field, new television contracts would be pouring billions of dollars into member schools' bank accounts, and on the field, nothing had changed: the SEC seemed to win the national championship every year. The world of college football was stable, with discussions about adding more schools to the playoff format seemingly the only controversial topic until a bombshell was dropped on the sport in the summer of 2021 in the scorching heat of Texas.

"Texas, Oklahoma Reach Out to SEC about Joining Conference," a headline screamed in the *Houston Chronicle*. Two of the biggest brands in college football were getting set to join the most powerful conference in the sport. The announcement sent shock waves from coast to coast. Administrators from both universities denied the reports initially, but less than a week later, both officially applied for membership in the

SEC. They will bring a combined 10 national championships in football when they begin play in the conference in the 2024–2025 academic year.

"The SEC has already established itself as the premier conference in collegiate athletics, and the addition of these two tradition-rich programs will make for an even more competitive conference in all sports," Alabama athletic director Greg Byrne said when the announcement was made.[11]

The additions of Texas and Oklahoma bring membership in the SEC to 16 institutions and represent the beginning of a new era for the conference. Only time will tell if the dominance on the gridiron will be maintained.

From 1936, when the AP began naming a national champion, through the 2005 college football season, the SEC won 11 titles. Throughout those 70 seasons, the Big Ten also brought home 11 titles. From 2006 through the 2023 season, the SEC has won 13 national championships in 17 seasons. The ACC has three, and the Big Ten has one. It has been an astonishing period of greatness for a single conference, an extraordinary stretch of supremacy that was decades in the making.

The SEC slogan proclaims that "it just means more." That is incomplete. Football in the SEC means everything.

Notes

Chapter 1

1. Tony Barnhart, *Southern Fried Football* (Chicago: Triumph Books, 2000), 116–17.
2. Christopher J. Walsh, *Where Football Is King* (Lanham, MD: Taylor Trade, 2006), 135.
3. Steve Irvine, "Alabama's 1926 Win in Rose Bowl Changed Football Landscape," *Birmingham News*, January 6, 2010.
4. Walsh, *Where Football Is King*, 135.
5. University of Alabama press release, "The Football Game That Changed the South," December 3, 1998.
6. Richard Scott, *SEC Football: 75 Years of Pride and Passion* (Minneapolis: Voyager Press, 2008), 31.
7. Matthew Gailani, "SEC: The Creation and Expansion of the Southeastern Conference," 2021, https://tnmuseum.org/Stories/posts/sec-the-creation-and-expansion-of-the-southeastern-conference?locale=en_us (accessed September 15, 2023).
8. Gailani, "SEC."
9. Walsh, *Where Football Is King*, 12.
10. Ray Glier, *How The SEC Became Goliath* (New York: Howard Books, 2012).
11. Walsh, *Where Football Is King*, 13.
12. Scott, *SEC Football*, 68.
13. Walsh, *Where Football Is King*, 107.
14. Scott, *SEC Football*, 53–55.
15. Barnhart, *Southern Fried Football*, 109.
16. Walsh, *Where Football Is King*, 109.
17. Barnhart, *Southern Fried Football*, 108.
18. Seth Emerson, "Journey Back to Sewanee, a Founding SEC Member That Has No Regrets," *The Athletic*, 2021, https://theathletic.com/2787563/2021/08/27/journey-back-to-sewanee-a-founding-sec-member-that-has-no-regrets (accessed September 15, 2023).

Chapter 2

1. Tony Barnhart, *Southern Fried Football* (Chicago: Triumph Books, 2000), 100.

2. Mark Bradley, "Fifty Years Ago, Georgia Tech Left the SEC," *Atlanta Journal-Constitution*, January 24, 2014.

3. Joe Minter, "Georgia Tech to Quit SEC Next January," *Atlanta Journal-Constitution*, July 21, 1963.

4. Mitchell Ginn, "The Day Georgia Tech Sports Changed Forever," *Georgia Tech Alumni Magazine*, February 24, 2011.

5. UPI Wire Service, "Georgia Tech Quits Conference," *New York Times*, January 25, 1964.

6. Alex Kirshner, "What If Louisiana Had Two SEC Teams All Along?," *Banner Society*, January 15, 2020, https://www.bannersociety.com/2020/1/15/21043678/tulane-lsu-football-history (accessed September 18, 2023).

7. Blake Toppmeyer, "Tulane Quits," *Clarion Ledger*, September 16, 2021, https://www.clarionledger.com/story/sports/college/ole-miss/2021/09/16/why-tulane-football-leave-sec-ole-miss-green-wave/8347963002 (accessed September 18, 2023).

8. Jude Papillion, "Why Tulane Left the SEC," *Tulane Hullabaloo*, September 23, 2022, https://tulanehullabaloo.com/61032/sports/why-tulane-left-the-sec (accessed September 18, 2023).

9. Joseph Durso, "Bear Bryant Is Dead at 69," *New York Times*, January 27, 1983.

10. Christopher J. Walsh, *Where Football Is King* (Lanham, MD: Taylor Trade, 2006), 28.

11. Ken Roberts, "The Bear Facts," *Tuscaloosa News*, September 11, 2018, https://www.tuscaloosanews.com/story/news/local/2018/09/11/coaching-legend-bear-bryant-was-born-105-years-ago/1079487100/ (accessed September 18, 2023).

12. Paul W. Bryant and John Underwood, *Bear: The Hard Life and Good Times of Alabama Coach Bryant* (Boston: Little, Brown, 1975), 48.

13. Bill Traughber, "Bear Bryant Was a Commodore," *Commodore History Corner*, September 7, 2006, https://vucommodores.com/chc-bear-bryant-was-a-commodore (accessed September 18, 2023).

14. Durso, "Bear Bryant Is Dead at 69."

15. Walsh, *Where Football Is King*, 139.

16. Richard Scott, *SEC Football: 75 Years of Pride and Passion* (Minneapolis: Voyager Press, 2008), 121.

17. Scott, *SEC Football*, 122.

18. Seth Emerson, "Grudges, Politics and Gentlemen's Agreements: The Chaotic History of SEC Scheduling," *The Athletic*, April 28, 2023 https://theathletic.com/4445067/2023/04/28/sec-schedule-history (accessed September 18, 2023).

19. Rick Cleveland, "Bama vs. Rebels, Bryant vs. Vaught," *Mississippi Today*, September 14, 2016, https://mississippitoday.org/2016/09/14/bama-vs-rebels-bryant-vs-vaught (accessed September 18, 2023).

20. Emerson, "Grudges, Politics and Gentlemen's Agreements."

21. Emerson, "Grudges, Politics and Gentlemen's Agreements."

22. Tom Shanahan, "Daugherty and Willie Ray Smith Sr. Courted Jerry LeVias to Board Underground Railroad," *Shanahan Report*, May 12, 2020, https://tomshanahan

.report/2020/05/daugherty-and-willie-ray-smith-sr-courted-jerry-levias-to-board-underground-railroad (accessed September 18, 2023).

23. Clifford F. Thies, "The Integration of College Football," *AIER*, September 23, 2021, https://www.aier.org/article/the-integration-of-college-football (accessed September 18, 2023).

24. Dave Kindred, "The Forgotten Trailblazer," *Sports on Earth*, November 5, 2013, https://web.archive.org/web/20150219031952/http://www.sportsonearth.com/article/63673094/nate-northington-sec-segregation-university-of-kentucky-ole-miss (accessed September 18, 2023).

25. Joel A. Erickson, "James Owens, the School's First Black Football Player, Leaves a Lasting Legacy at Auburn with Award Named for Him," *AL.com*, September 13, 2012, https://www.al.com/auburnfootball/2012/09/james_owens_the_schools_first.html (accessed September 18, 2023).

26. Phillip Marshall, "Demeanor, Abilities Helped Jackson Win Over Tide Fans," *Gadsden Times*, July 23, 2006.

27. Kindred, "The Forgotten Trailblazer."

CHAPTER 3

1. Keith Dunnavant, *The 50 Year Seduction* (New York: Thomas Dunne Books, 2004), 7.

2. Dunnavant, *The 50 Year Seduction*, 8.

3. Dunnavant, *The 50 Year Seduction*, 8.

4. Dunnavant, *The 50 Year Seduction*, 9.

5. Steve Spurrier and Buddy Martin, *Head Ball Coach: My Life in Football* (New York: Blue Rider Press, 2016), 57.

6. Spurrier and Martin, *Head Ball Coach*, 66.

7. Spurrier and Martin, *Head Ball Coach*, 66.

8. Spurrier and Martin, *Head Ball Coach*, 64.

9. Spurrier and Martin, *Head Ball Coach*, 67.

10. AP Wire, "Crimson Tide Called Best by P. Bryant," *Anniston Star*, October 25, 1964.

11. Spurrier and Martin, *Head Ball Coach*, 76.

12. Dunnavant, *The 50 Year Seduction*, 110.

13. Dunnavant, *The 50 Year Seduction*, 110.

14. Gordon S. White Jr., "N.C.A.A. Reorganizes into 3 Groups," *New York Times*, August 7, 1973.

15. Dunnavant, *The 50 Year Seduction*, 111.

16. Dunnavant, *The 50 Year Seduction*, 112.

17. "84 NCAA Supreme Court Case . . . 30 Years Later," *WVU Sports*, https://wvusports.com/news/2014/7/11/25935_131465989211764928 (accessed September 18, 2023).

18. Dunnavant, *The 50 Year Seduction*, 123.

19. Gordon S. White Jr., "Rival Football Unit Approves TV Pact," *New York Times*, August 22, 1981.

20. John Underwood, "To Do Over What to Do," *Sports Illustrated*, September 21, 1981.

21. "The 5-Year-Old College Football Association Meets in Atlanta on Friday," *UPI*, August 20, 1981.

22. Gordon S. White Jr., "N.C.A.A. Calls Convention on TV Policy," *New York Times*, September 9, 1981.

23. Christopher J. Walsh, *Where Football Is King* (Lanham, MD: Taylor Trade, 2006), 77.

24. Jeff Sentell, "The Absolutely Unbelievable Coin Flip Herschel Walker Recruiting Story," *Dawg Nation*, https://www.dawgnation.com/football/recruiting/the-absolutely -coin-flip-unbelievable-herschel-walker-recruiting-story (accessed September 18, 2023).

25. Richard Scott, *SEC Football: 75 Years of Pride and Passion* (Minneapolis: Voyager Press, 2008), 178.

26. Barry Tramel, "OU, Georgia Changed College Football with Its Lawsuit against the NCAA," *The Oklahoman*, December 23, 2017.

27. Tramel, "OU, Georgia Changed College Football with Its Lawsuit against the NCAA."

28. Tramel, "OU, Georgia Changed College Football with Its Lawsuit against the NCAA."

29. Dunnavant, *The 50 Year Seduction*, 160.

30. Tim Tucker, "UGA Helped End NCAA's TV Monopoly," *Atlanta Journal-Constitution*, August 29, 2010.

CHAPTER 4

1. Bob Sims, "Schiller Moved SEC to the Front," *AL.com*, July 25, 2007, https://www.al .com/bn/2007/07/schiller_moved_sec_to_the_front.html (accessed September 19, 2023).

2. Keith Dunnavant, *The 50 Year Seduction* (New York: Thomas Dunne Books, 2004), 97.

3. Dunnavant, *The 50 Year Seduction*, 173.

4. Mark Asher, "Despite TV Fuss, College Grid Solid," *Washington Post*, August 26, 1984.

5. Dunnavant, *The 50 Year Seduction*, 179.

6. Mike Mulhurn, "Football on TV: Stay Tuned," *Winston-Salem Journal*, August 24, 1984.

7. Christopher J. Walsh, *Where Football Is King* (Lanham, MD: Taylor Trade, 2006), 29.

8. Dwayne Cox, "The Depression and World War II," *Auburn Archives*.

9. Tony Barnhart, *Southern Fried Football* (Chicago: Triumph Books, 2000), 105.

10. AP, "Tigers Get Grid Award," *St. Petersburg Times*, December 10, 1957.

11. ESPN, *Saturdays in the South: A History of SEC Football*, episode 5, September 1, 2022.

12. ESPN, *Saturdays in the South*.

13. Cecil Hurt, "Bo Has Respect of Bama Frosh," *Tuscaloosa News*, November 21, 1985.

14. Barnhart, *Southern Fried Football*, 59.

15. Dunnavant, *The 50 Year Seduction*, 185.

16. Dunnavant, *The 50 Year Seduction*, 185.

17. Dunnavant, *The 50 Year Seduction*, 181.

18. Barry Lasswell, "ACC Was Second Choice," *Anderson Independent Mail*, June 4, 1978.

19. Blake Toppemeyer, "How the SEC Tried to Add Texas Longhorns More Than 30 Years Ago," *The Tennessean*, August 16, 2021.

20. Jack Hairston, "A 16 Team SEC?," *Gainesville Sun*, April 11, 1989.

21. Hairston, "A 16 Team SEC?"

22. Jack Hairston, "SEC Expansion Is Probably Years Away," *Gainesville Sun*, May 20, 1989.

23. AP Wire, "SEC, Miami Interested in Talking," *Waycross Journal-Herald*, May 11, 1989.

24. AP Wire, "SEC, Miami Interested in Talking."

25. Wire Reports, "FSU's Bowden Doubts SEC Expansion Stories," *Albany Herald*, July 23, 1989.

26. David Jones, "Welcome to the Big Ten," *Penn Live*, July 23, 2013.

27. Jones, "Welcome to the Big Ten."

28. David Jones, "How Penn State Nearly Ended Up in ACC," *Penn Live*, September 14, 2020.

29. Jones, "How Penn State Nearly Ended Up in ACC."

30. Jones, "Welcome to the Big Ten."

31. Jones, "How Penn State Nearly Ended Up in ACC."

32. Mark Wogenrich, "Big Ten Expansion, Penn State and the Future," *All Penn State*, August 5, 2023.

33. Toppemeyer, "How the SEC Tried to Add Texas Longhorns More Than 30 Years Ago."

34. Toppemeyer, "How the SEC Tried to Add Texas Longhorns More Than 30 Years Ago."

35. Sam Khan Jr., "The Demise of the Southwest Conference," *ESPN*, December 2, 2020.

36. Khan, "The Demise of the Southwest Conference."

37. Khan, "The Demise of the Southwest Conference."

38. Toppemeyer, "How the SEC Tried to Add Texas Longhorns More Than 30 Years Ago."

39. Khan, "The Demise of the Southwest Conference."

40. AP Wire, "Broyles' Tone Sounds Good to SWC," *Victoria Advocate*, July 13, 1990.

41. AP Wire, "Arkansas Ready to Join SEC," *Orlando Sentinel*, July 31, 1990.

42. Khan, "The Demise of the Southwest Conference."

43. NDJRS, "Notre Dame Is Partly Responsible for Arkansas Being in the SEC," *One Foot Down*, August 3, 2020.

44. NDJRS, "Notre Dame Is Partly Responsible for Arkansas Being in the SEC."

45. Gene Wojchiechowski, "Florida State Reverse Was the Right Play," *Los Angeles Times*, September 20, 1990.

46. Steven Wine, "Miami Decides against Joining the SEC," *Los Angeles Times*, September 26, 1990.

47. SI Staff, "Storming into the Big East," *Sports Illustrated*, October 22, 1990.

48. Ben Portnoy, How SEC Landed on South Carolina," *The State*, September 8, 2022.

CHAPTER 5

1. Chris Low, "How the 1992 SEC Championship Game Altered the College Football Landscape Forever," *ESPN*, August 18, 2022.

2. AP Wire, "UT Clinches SEC with Win over Vandy," *Knoxville Daily News*, December 1, 1985.

3. Low, "How the 1992 SEC Championship Game Altered the College Football Landscape Forever."

4. Ray Glier, *How The SEC Became Goliath* (New York: Howard Books, 2012), 36.

5. Allen Barra, *The Last Coach* (New York: Norton, 2005), 485.

6. Tom Callahan, "Tears Fall on Alabama," *Time*, February 7, 1983.

7. Richard Scott, *SEC Football: 75 Years of Pride and Passion* (Minneapolis: Voyager Press, 2008), 174.

8. Bill Curry, "DuBose Never Met Expectations This Season," *ESPN*, December 8, 1999.

9. Richard Scott, "Stallings a Lot Like Bear Bryant," *Birmingham Post-Herald*, January 10, 1990.

10. Mark McCarter, "Kramer to Begin Piecing Together Expanded SEC," *Anniston Star*, October 16, 1990.

11. AP Wire, "Cities Make Bid for SEC Title Game," *Dothan Eagle*, February 20, 1991.

12. Joey Johnston, "Tampa among Cities Seeking SEC Title Game," *Tampa Tribune*, February 6, 1991.

13. Mike Bianchi, "Orlando Makes Strong Bid for SEC Title Game," *Florida Today*, February 19, 1991.

14. Bianchi, "Orlando Makes Strong Bid For SEC Title Game."

15. Jeremy Gray, "Iron Bowl 1964 Was the First Nationally Televised," *AL.com*, https://www.al.com/news/birmingham/2014/11/iron_bowl_64_was_first_nationa.html (accessed September 20, 2023).

16. Creg Stephenson, "We'll Play '89 in Auburn," *AL.com*, https://www.al.com/sports/2019/11/well-play-89-in-auburn-how-pat-dye-helped-break-birminghams-40-year-iron-bowl-stranglehold.html (accessed September 20, 2023).

17. Stephenson, "We'll Play '89 in Auburn."

18. Phillip Marshall, "AU Wants Tide in Jordan-Hare," *Montgomery Advertiser*, December 9, 1984.

19. Marshall, "AU Wants Tide In Jordan-Hare."

20. AP Wire, "Sloan May Avoid Dispute with AU," *Birmingham Post-Herald*, February 7, 1987.

21. Stephenson, "We'll Play '89 in Auburn."

22. Stephenson, "We'll Play '89 in Auburn."

23. George Diaz, "SEC Title Game under Attack," *Orlando Sentinel*, June 12, 1991.

24. Gary Lundy, "SEC's End of Season Football Playoff May Meet Challenge," *Pensacola News Journal*, May 2, 1991.

25. Bill Kaczor, "Birmingham Gets Vote for SEC Game," *Johnson City Press*, May 31, 1991.

26. Hoyt Harwell, "SEC to Begin Divisional Play," *Newnan-Times Herald*, December 11, 1990.

27. Bill King, "SEC: Is It Too Tough for a National Title," *Gainesville Sun*, July 30, 1992.

28. Keith Dunnavant, *The 50 Year Seduction* (New York: Thomas Dunne Books, 2004), 243.

29. Larry Flemming, "SEC Tie-Breaking Rules Undecided," *Chattanooga Times*, December 13, 1991.

30. AP Wire, "Gators and Spurrier Near Contract," *The Tennessean*, December 14, 1989.

31. Steve Spurrier and Buddy Martin, *Head Ball Coach: My Life in Football* (New York: Blue Rider Press, 2016), 145.

32. Spurrier and Martin, *Head Ball Coach*, 162.

33. Mike Knobler, "National Title beyond SEC Teams Reach," *Jackson Clarion-Ledger*, July 30, 1992.

34. Jimmy Smyth, "SEC Coaches Talk Titles, Expansion," *Johnson City Press*, July 30, 1992.

35. Scott, *SEC Football*, 192.

36. Doug Nye, "ABC, NBC Have Interest in SEC Championship Game," *The State*, December 5, 1992.

37. Low, "How the 1992 SEC Championship Game Altered the College Football Landscape Forever."

38. Dunnavant, *The 50 Year Seduction*.

39. Low, "How the 1992 SEC Championship Game Altered the College Football Landscape Forever."

CHAPTER 6

1. Keith Dunnavant, *The 50 Year Seduction* (New York: Thomas Dunne Books, 2004), 206.

2. Wendell Barnhouse, "College Football Looking to Taste Bigger Slice of Television Rights Pie," *Fort Worth Star Telegram*, March 6, 1989.

3. AP Wire, "ABC Takes CFA Package from CBS," *Birmingham Post-Herald*, January 18, 1990.

4. Dunnavant, *The 50 Year Seduction*, 211.

5. Dunnavant, *The 50 Year Seduction*, 216.

6. Jack Craig, "NBC-ND Deal Makes Waves," *Boston Globe*, February 6, 1990.

7. Ed Sherman, "Notre Dame Deal With NBC Stirs Furor," *Chicago Tribune*, February 6, 1990.

8. Dunnavant, *The 50 Year Seduction*, 216.

9. Terence Moore, "NBC Deal Has Irish Fighting More Criticism," *Atlanta Journal-Constitution*, February 10, 1990.

10. Allan Crow, "SEC May Get Its Own TV Package," *Shreveport Journal*, February 9, 1990.

11. Dunnavant, *The 50 Year Seduction*, 222.

12. Dunnavant, *The 50 Year Seduction*, 222.

13. Jim Benson, "NBC, NFL Shut Out CBS," *Variety*, December 20, 1993.

14. Bryan Curtis, "The Great NFL Heist: How Fox Paid for and Changed Football Forever," *The Ringer*, December 13, 2018.

15. Ivan Maisel, "SEC's plan raises anger from CFA," *Dallas Morning News*, February 3, 1994.

16. Wendell Barnhouse, "SEC-CBS Talks Leave Other CFA Schools Anxious, Angry," *Fort Worth Star-Telegram*, February 6, 1994.

17. Bob Sims, "How The Southeastern Conference Got Rich," *AL.com*, February 24, 2008.

18. AP Wire, "CBS Fills Big Hole with SEC Contract," *Odessa American*, February 12, 1994.

19. Tim Peeler, "ACC Believes TV a Danger in Future," *Greenville News*, June 26, 1994.

20. Dan Wolken, "Lloyd Landesman and the Sound That Makes the SEC on CBS," *USA Today*, December 6, 2013.

21. Wolken, "Lloyd Landesman and The Sound That Makes the SEC on CBS."

22. Verne Lundquist, *Play by Play* (New York: HarperCollins, 2018), 203.

23. Lundquist, *Play by Play*, 205.

24. Richard Scott, *SEC Football: 75 Years of Pride and Passion* (Minneapolis: Voyager Press, 2008), 190.

25. Paul Finebaum, "SEC Wasn't Impressed With The Birmingham Football Foundation," *Birmingham Post-Herald*, 25 February 25, 1994.

26. Steve Spurrier and Buddy Martin, *Head Ball Coach: My Life In Football* (New York: Blue Rider Press, 2016), 171.

27. Spurrier and Martin, *Head Ball Coach*, 177.

28. Spurrier and Martin, *Head Ball Coach*, 179.

29. Spurrier and Martin, *Head Ball Coach*, 187.

CHAPTER 7

1. Jack Doane, "Rebounding Rebels Face Alabama," *Montgomery Advertiser*, October 4, 1969.

2. Christopher J. Walsh, *Where Football Is King* (Lanham, MD: Taylor Trade, 2006), 184.

3. Jack Doane, "Tide Outlasts Rebels 33–32," *Montgomery Advertiser*, October 5, 1969.

4. SEC Network, *SEC Storied: The Book of Manning*, season 1, episode 10, September 24, 2014.

5. SEC Network, "*SEC Storied*."

6. Richard Scott, *SEC Football: 75 Years of Pride and Passion* (Minneapolis: Voyager Press, 2008), 145.

7. Walsh, *Where Football Is King*, 198.

8. Tony Barnhart, *Southern Fried Football* (Chicago: Triumph Books, 2000), 115.

9. Chris Wuench, "How Peyton Manning Came to Choose Tennessee over Ole Miss," *Saturday Down South*, https://www.saturdaydownsouth.com/tennessee-football/how-peyton-came-to-choose-tennessee-over-ole-miss (accessed September 25, 2023).

NOTES

10. Jimmy Hyams, "Peyton Manning Commits to Tennessee," *Knoxville News-Sentinel*, December 3, 1994.

11. Kevin Duffy, "Peyton Manning Mulled Michigan," *Mass Live*, https://www.masslive.com/patriots/2014/10/peyton_manning_tom_brady_rival.html (accessed September 25, 2023).

12. Scott, *SEC Football*, 200.

13. Fred Goodall, "Manning Leaves Disappointed," *Leaf-Chronicle*, September 21, 1997.

14. Walsh, *Where Football Is King*, 28.

15. John Zenor, "Manning Has Eyes on Prize," *Montgomery Advertiser*, December 5, 1997.

16. Thomas Stinson, "Manning Delivers," *Atlanta Journal-Constitution*, December 7, 1997.

17. Christoper Kamrani, "How to Land Archie Manning," *The Athletic*, May 22, 2022, https://theathletic.com/3252703/2022/05/11/arch-manning-recruitment-peyton-manning-eli-manning (accessed September 25, 2023).

18. Knight Ridder, "A Can't Miss Prospect," *New York Daily News*, December 20, 1998.

19. Kamrani, "How to Land Archie Manning."

20. Sekou Smith, "Eli's Coming to Ole Miss," *Jackson Clarion-Ledger*, December 19, 1998.

21. Kamrani, "How to Land Archie Manning."

22. AP Wire, "Mannings Enjoy Day at Swamp," *Hattiesburg American*, October 5, 2003.

23. SEC Network, *SEC Storied*.

24. Ron Higgins, "The Father of the BCS," *Allstate Sugar Bowl Program*, 2014.

25. Higgins, "The Father of the BCS."

26. Andy Staples, "The Chaos and Controversy of the BCS," *Sports Illustrated*, July 9, 2018.

27. Keith Dunnavant, *The 50 Year Seduction* (New York: Thomas Dunne Books, 2004), 255.

28. Staples, "The Chaos and Controversy of the BCS."

29. Charles Bennett, "Inside the Minds of the Men Who Invented the BCS," *Bleacher Report*, November 24, 2013.

30. Bennett, "Inside the Minds of the Men Who Invented the BCS."

31. Bennett, "Inside the Minds of the Men Who Invented the BCS."

32. Bennett, "Inside the Minds of the Men Who Invented the BCS."

33. Bob Baum, "Priceless Performance by Peerless," *Vero Beach Press Journal*, January 5, 1999.

34. Baum, "Priceless Performance by Peerless."

35. Geoff Calkins, "If That's Ugly, We Love Ugly," *Memphis Commercial Appeal*, January 5, 1999.

36. Richard Sandomir, "CBS Is Being Beaten by ABC," *New York Times*, November 26, 1996.

37. Sandomir, "CBS Is Being Beaten by ABC."

38. Doug Nye, " Deal with CBS Will Increase SEC's Exposure," *State*, February 7, 1998.

39. Joe Reedy, "How Fox's 25 Seasons of Covering the NFL Changed the Game," *AP News*, https://apnews.com.article/9816ca0d0b3546ac92353c655d40cab8 (accessed September 26, 2023).

40. Prentis Rogers, "Duke-UNC Faces Tough Competition," *Atlanta Journal-Constitution*, February 4, 1998.

41. David Wassan, "Money, Exposure, Outweigh Flaws of SEC's TV Deals," *Tuscaloosa News*, June 12, 2005.

42. John Zenor, "Commissioner of SEC to Retire," *Sun Herald*, March 13, 2002.

43. AP Wire, "Kramer's 'Great Ride' Is Over," *The Tennessean*, March 13, 2002.

44. AP Wire, "Slive Named Southeastern Conference Commissioner," *SEC Sports*, July 2, 2002.

CHAPTER 8

1. Press Release, "Skipper Heard Had Lasting Impact on LSU Athletics," *LSUSports.net*, https://lsusports.net/news/2019/07/11/205174318-2 (accessed September 26, 2023).

2. Christopher J. Walsh, *Where Football Is King* (Lanham, MD: Taylor Trade, 2006), 198.

3. Richard Scott, *SEC Football: 75 Years of Pride and Passion* (Minneapolis: Voyager Press, 2008), 105.

4. Walsh, *Where Football Is King*, 182.

5. Ray Glier, *How the SEC Became Goliath* (New York: Howard Books, 2012), 80.

6. Glier, *How the SEC Became Goliath*, 82.

7. Walsh, *Where Football Is King*, 186.

8. Scott Ferrell, "Coach Brings Impressive Credentials," *Shreveport Times*, December 1, 1999.

9. Ross Delinger, "Skyler Green, Nick Saban, Laser Pick," *SI.com*, October 9, 2018, https://www.si.com/college/2018/10/09/lsu-georgia-2003-nick-saban-skyler-green (accessed September 27, 2023).

10. Delinger, "Skyler Green, Nick Saban, Laser Pick."

11. Tony Barnhart, "LSU Won the Physical Battle," *Atlanta Journal-Constitution*, December 7, 2003.

12. Paul Newberry, "LSU States Its Case for No. 2," *Anniston Star*, December 7, 2003.

13. Roy Lang III, "Title Is Huge for LSU," *Shreveport Times*, January 5, 2004.

14. Lang, "Title Is Huge for LSU."

15. Zach Ragan, "Nick Saban Nearly Screwed Up LSU Football's 2003 National Championship," *Death Valley Voice*, https://deathvalleyvoice.com/2020/05/06/lsu-football-nick-saban-nearly-screwed-tigers (accessed September 28, 2023).

16. AP Wire, "Spurrier Resigns as Gators Coach," *ESPN*, January 5, 2002.

17. Kevin Flaherty, "Urban Meyer Discusses Why He Picked Florida over Notre Dame," *247 Sports*, https://247sports.com/Article/Urban-Meyer-Ohio-State-Buckeyes-football-Florida-Gators-Notre-Dame-Fighting-Irish-favorite-season-Utah-134707969 (accessed September 28, 2023).

18. Flaherty, "Urban Meyer Discusses Why He Picked Florida over Notre Dame."

19. Antonya English, "Gators Get What They Want in Meyer," *St. Petersburg Times*, December 5, 2004.

20. David Jones, "Meyer Brings Potent Offense to Gators," *Florida Today*, December 4, 2004.

21. Glier, *How the SEC Became Goliath*, 44.

22. Ari Wasserman, "Urban Meyer Reflects on Maniacal Pursuit of Talent," *The Athletic*, March 1, 2023, https://theathletic.com/4260106/2023/03/01/urban-meyer-recruiting-qa -florida-ohio-state (accessed September 29, 2023).

23. Wasserman, "Urban Meyer Reflects on Maniacal Pursuit of Talent."

24. Jeff Schultz, "Gators Need More to Jump Michigan," *Atlanta Journal-Constitution*, December 3, 2006.

25. AP Wire, "Michigan's Carr Calls Tressel's Abstinence from Voting 'Slick,'" *Detroit Free-Press*, December 4, 2006.

26. AP Wire, "Gators Attack: Florida Gets Title with Rout of Ohio State," *ESPN*, August 28, 2007.

CHAPTER 9

1. Griffin McVeigh, "Urban Meyer Recalls Story from Tim Tebow Recruitment," *On3*, June 10, 2023, https://www.on3.com/college/florida-gators/news/tim-tebow-recruitment -alabama-head-coach-urban-meyer (accessed September 29, 2023).

2. Patrick Pinack, "One Phone Call Nearly Brought Tim Tebow to Alabama," *Fan Buzz*, February 24, 2023, https://fanbuzz.com/college-football/sec/tim-tebow -recruitment-phone-call (accessed September 29, 2023).

3. Pinack, "One Phone Call Nearly Brought Tim Tebow to Alabama."

4. Buddy Martin, "It's Tim Tebow's Team as Gators Get Set for '07," *Port Charlotte Sun*, August 12, 2007.

5. Mark Maske, "LSU's Saban Accepts Offer to Coach Dolphins," *Washington Post*, December 26, 2004.

6. Greg Stoda, "Tebow Apologizes, but Meyer to Blame," *Palm Beach Post*, September 28, 2008.

7. Pinack, "One Phone Call Nearly Brought Tim Tebow To Alabama."

8. Ari Wasserman, "Urban Meyer Reflects on Maniacal Pursuit of Talent," *The Athletic*, March 1, 2023, https://theathletic.com/4260106/2023/03/01/urban-meyer-recruiting-qa -florida-ohio-state (accessed September 29, 2023).

9. Kyle Veazey, "Rebs Boone Sees Exposure for UM, MSU," *Clarion Ledger*, August 15, 2008.

10. John Zenor, "SEC, ESPN Sign 15-Year Deal," *Pensacola News-Journal*, August 26, 2008.

11. Ron Higgins, "SEC Cashes In on ESPN Exposure," *Commercial Appeal*, August 26, 2008.

12. Tony Barnhart, "SEC Rakes In Billions with New ESPN Contract," *The State*, August 26, 2008.

13. Press Release, "College Football Continues to Build Unprecedented Interest," *Military Bowl*, March 23, 2011, https://militarybowl.org/college-football-continues

-to-build-unprecedented-intere t-with-record-attendance-and-stellar-ratings (accessed September 29, 2023).

14. Chris Hummer, "Nick Saban Q&A," *247 Sports*, https://247sports.com/longformarticle/nick-saban-bryce-young-nil-7-figure-deal-qa-drew-brees-retirement-defensive-changes-168011837/#1672702 (accessed September 29, 2023).

15. Brian Stultz, "Steve Spurrier Turned Down Alabama Job Offer," *Stadium*, April 20, 2016.

16. John Talty, "Looking Back at What Really Happened between Alabama and Rich Rodriguez," *AL.com*, December 3, 2016, https://www.al.com/alabamafootball/2016/12/looking_back_at_what_really_ha.html (accessed September 29, 2023).

17. Tim Gayle, "Tide Lands Big Fish," *Montgomery Advertiser*, January 4, 2007.

18. Lars Anderson, *Chasing the Bear* (New York: Grand Central Publishing, 2019), 31.

19. Chase Goodbread, "A Reminder This Alabama Dynasty Began with RichRod," *Tuscaloosa News*, April 13, 2022.

20. Anderson, *Chasing the Bear*, 34

21. Creg Stephenson, "Saban the Day," *Aniston Star*, January 4, 2007.

22. Mike Tankersley, "Saban Takes Command," *Montgomery Advertiser*, January 5, 2007.

23. Glenn Guilbeau, "Saban's Wife Knows Talent Too," *Shreveport Times*, December 5, 2009.

24. Andrea Adelson, "Prelude to BCS," *Orlando Sentinel*, December 5, 2009.

CHAPTER 10

1. Bob Murphy, "Head on the Sportrola," *Knoxville Journal*, December 10, 1932.

2. Michael Casagrande, "Part Deux," *Montgomery Advertiser*, December 5, 2011.

3. Michael Rosenberg, "Alabama Overmatches Notre Dame in Joke of a Title Game," *Sports Illustrated*, January 7, 2013.

4. Dave Wilson, "How Texas A&M and the SEC Formed a Perfect Fit," *ESPN.com*, July 21, 2021, https://www.espn.com/college-football/story/_/id/31845340/how-texas-sec-college-football-top-conference-formed-perfect-fit (accessed September 29, 2023).

5. Wilson, "How Texas A&M and the SEC Formed a Perfect Fit."

6. Lars Anderson, *Chasing the Bear* (New York: Grand Central Publishing, 2019), 36.

7. Seth Emerson, "The Cost to Compete," *The Athletic*, February 6, 2020, https://theathletic.com/1590155/2020/02/06/georgia-recruiting-national-footprint-impact-budget (accessed September 29, 2023).

8. Seth Emerson, "A Bigger Spotlight," *Macon Telegraph*, May 3, 2013.

9. Press Release, "SEC and ESPN Reach Milestone Agreement," *SEC Sports*, December 10, 2020.

10. Andrew Olsen, "ESPN Exec Address Status of 'SEC on CBS' Music," *Saturday Down South*, https://www.saturdaydownsouth.com/sec-football/sec-on-cbs-music-theme-song-espn-abc-tv-deal (accessed September 29, 2023).

11. Paul Weber, "SEC Welcomes Texas, Oklahoma after Boards Accept Invitations," *AP News*, July 30, 2021.

Select Bibliography

Anderson, Lars. *Chasing The Bear*. New York: Grand Central Publishing, 2019.

Barnhart, Tony. *Southern Fried Football*. Chicago: Triumph Books, 2000.

Barra, Allen. *The Last Coach*. New York: Norton, 2005.

Bryant, Paul W., and John Underwood. *Bear: The Hard Life and Good Times of Alabama Coach Bryant*. Boston: Little, Brown, 1975.

Dunnavant, Keith. *The 50 Year Seduction*. New York: Thomas Dunne Books, 2004.

Glier, Ray. *How The SEC Became Goliath*. New York: Howard Books, 2012.

Lundquist, Verne. *Play by Play*. New York: HarperCollins, 2018.

Scott, Richard. *SEC Football: 75 Years of Pride and Passion*. Minneapolis: Voyager Press, 2008.

Spurrier, Steve, and Buddy Martin. *Head Ball Coach: My Life in Football*. New York: Blue Rider Press, 2016.

Walsh, Christopher J. *Where Football Is King*. Lanham, MD: Taylor Trade, 2006.

INDEX

About the Author

Colby Newton has covered college football and worked in the college football world for more than 20 years. As a college student in the early days of the internet, he founded a college football website, leading to hundreds of guest appearances on radio programs all over the country. Spending more than a decade in the bowl game industry, he had the privilege of standing on the sidelines at multiple Sugar, Holiday, Gator, and Alamo bowls. Colby has written for *Lindy's College Football* and the *Deseret News* and authored a book about the Utah–BYU rivalry. He lives in the Salt Lake City suburb of Draper, Utah, with his wife and five children and dreams of someday retiring in SEC country near a backwoods Tennessee byway.

www.ingramcontent.com/pod-product-compliance
Lightning Source LLC
Chambersburg PA
CBHW030306100426
42812CB00002B/592